Amish-Inspired Quilts

Tradition with a Piece O' Cake Twist

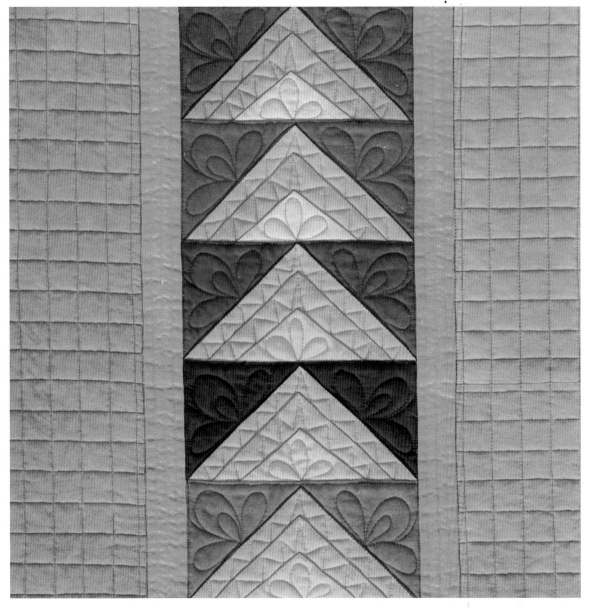

BECKY GOLDSMITH & LINDA JENKINS

C&T PUBLISHING

Text and Artwork © 2006 Becky Goldsmith and Linda Jenkins

Artwork © 2006 C&T Publishing, Inc.

Publisher: Amy Marson

Editorial Director: Gailen Runge

Acquisitions Editor: Jan Grigsby

Editor: Lynn Koolish

Technical Editors: Gayl Gallagher, Nanette Zeller

Copyeditor/Proofreader: Wordfirm, Inc.

Cover Designer: Christina Jarumay

Production Artist: Kirstie L. Pettersen

Illustrators: Becky Goldsmith and Tim Manibusan

Production Assistant: Matt Allen

Photography: Luke Mulks unless otherwise noted

Published by C&T Publishing, Inc., P.O. Box 1456, Lafayette, CA 94549

Library of Congress Cataloging-in-Publication Data

Goldsmith, Becky,

  Amish-inspired quilts : tradition with a Piece O' Cake twist / Becky
Goldsmith and Linda Jenkins.

    p. cm.

  Includes index.

  ISBN 1-57120-334-6 (paper trade)

  1. Patchwork--Patterns. 2. Quilting--Patterns. 3. Quilts, Amish. I.
Jenkins, Linda, II. Piece O'Cake Designs. III. Title.

  TT835.G654493 2006

  746.46'041--dc22

                    2005017044

Printed in China   10 9 8 7 6 5 4 3 2 1

Table of Contents

Acknowledgments

We are very lucky to be associated with C&T. Everyone there has been very good to us. First, Todd Hensley, CEO, welcomed us with open arms. Amy Marson, publisher, is always there to support us. Lynn Koolish, our editor, helps us make each book the best it can be. We thank them all.

It would be nice to be perfect, but we aren't, so we are very grateful to Gayl Gallagher, our technical editor, who makes sure that we get the details right. Luke Mulks, our photographer, makes everything look beautiful. Kirstie Pettersen, this book's graphic artist, has given *Amish-Inspired Quilts* its distinctive appearance. Christina Jarumay designed a fabulous cover. Matt Allen, the production assistant, kept everything running smoothly. We thank you all for your excellent efforts.

Amish quilts and solid fabrics go hand in hand. We are sincerely grateful to Primrose Gradations and Cherrywood Fabrics for the hand-dyed solids that we used in our quilts.

We owe a special word of thanks to Rachel Pellman, who encouraged us to pursue the idea that this book is based on.

Dedication

From Becky

Our sons, Christopher and Jeff, are good boys—men now. They talk to me, sharing what's going on in their lives—I love that! It's great to brag about their accomplishments, but I find that what I like the most are the everyday conversations we have. Our oldest son, Christopher, is married. His wife, Lorna, is a joy to have in the family—and she talks to me too! Their daughter, Elanor, is three and doing her best to join in now.

The boys have always expressed an appreciation for the quilts that I make. But they really, *really* like the quilts in this book. As a new one went up on the design wall, one or the other would lay claim to it. *Lorna's Vine* is hanging in Christopher and Lorna's dining room!

Quilts are a tangible expression of love. I give my quilts to members of my family, hoping that they feel the love that goes into them. It makes me happy knowing how much the kids already treasure their quilts.

Christopher and Jeff

From Linda

My sister, Judy, is the best sister anyone could have and she is also my best friend. She lives far away but we find ways to spend time together. We are always together at Christmas. All I have to say is "road trip" and she is there.

The family describes her as the sweet, calm, gentle, spirited sister. They never use those words to describe me. Through good times and bad she has always been there for me. Judy loves my quilts and is always so encouraging.

I wish everyone could have the opportunity to know her. She is a gift from God for me.

Linda and Judy

Introduction

Amish quilts grew out of the Amish religious tradition. As a people, the Amish live separately from the culture at large, finding meaning in a simpler lifestyle in small communities of faith.

We know the Amish by their quilts. The women inside an Amish community often shared piecing and quilting patterns with each other. Sometimes patterns would be shared between women from different communities. In this way designs spread through Amish communities, across the United States.

Amish quilts are most often pieced and the designs are usually simple. Their beauty comes from the way each individual quilter used color in her quilts. The solid fabrics in these quilts are plain—free from pattern. But solid fabrics don't have to be dull or quiet. Many Amish quilts are made from rich, bright, wonderful colors.

There are often large open spaces in Amish quilts. Wide, plain borders act as a mat does around a photograph. These spaces, filled with quilting, compel you to focus on the pieced design in the quilt.

We have always loved Amish quilts, but we love appliqué too! The Amish did very little appliqué before 1940. It is true that there were some individuals who decided to follow a different path, occasionally making an appliqué quilt, but antique Amish appliqué quilts are rare.

We began to wonder: What if the Amish had done more appliqué? What would it look like? Would these quilters have filled the open spaces with appliqué to balance the piecing? Would they have *substituted* appliqué for the piecing, preserving the open spaces in the quilt? We imagined that they might have done both, as you'll see from our quilts in this book.

As we worked on our quilts, we couldn't help but notice how contemporary they look. Our brand-new fabric, untouched by time, is part of the reason why this is true. Then we looked again at antique Amish quilts. In many cases, if you take these quilts out of context, they look very modern. The piecing designs in Amish quilts do not have a dated look; we still use them today. Solid fabrics don't look dated the way a very old print does. Our quilts will feel more antique as the fabric in them ages, the same way it has in the older, Amish quilts.

We had an inspiration while designing the quilts for this book. Some old quilts have been loved and used so much that only bits of them are left. These leftover bits may be only a fraction of what the whole quilt once was, but many are quite interesting standing alone. You'll find eight fragments designed especially for this book starting on page 35.

We really enjoyed working in the Amish tradition, and we hope that you do as well.

Basic Supplies

Fabric: All the fabrics used in these quilts are 100% cotton. We used hand-dyed solids for our quilts. Solids off the bolt will work as well. Always prewash your cotton fabric.

Appliqué thread: Use cotton thread with cotton fabric. There are many brands to choose from. Work with different brands until you find the one that works best for you. For hand appliqué, we can recommend DMC 50-weight machine embroidery thread, Aurifil 50-weight cotton thread, and Mettler 60-weight machine embroidery thread. All of these are 2-ply threads.

Machine quilting thread: Use cotton thread with cotton fabric. We most often use the thread listed above for our machine quilting. We like a lot of quilting in our quilts, so this works well. If you plan for your quilting lines to be far apart, you should use a heavier thread.

Hand quilting thread: Use cotton thread with cotton fabric. We like Gütermann's hand quilting thread.

Pins: Use ½" sequin pins to pin the appliqué pieces in place. Use larger flower-head quilting pins to hold the positioning overlay in place where necessary.

Needles: For hand appliqué, we use a size 11 Hemming & Son milliner's needle. There are many good needles. Find the one that fits **your** hand.

Scissors: Use embroidery-size scissors for both paper and fabric. Small, sharp scissors are better for intricate cutting.

Rotary cutter, mat, and acrylic ruler: When trimming blocks to size and cutting borders, rotary cutting tools will give you the best results.

X-ACTO knife: This is a very precise tool to use to cut quilting pattern stencils.

Pencils: We use either a General's Charcoal White pencil or an Ultimate Mechanical Pencil for Quilters to draw around templates onto the fabric. To mark quilting lines, we use either of the pencils mentioned above. You might also try Roxanne's silver pencil or Clover's Fine White Marking Pen. Test any pencil on your fabrics to be sure that you can see it and remove it.

Permanent markers: To make the positioning overlay, a Sharpie Ultra Fine Point Permanent Marker works best on the upholstery vinyl.

Clear upholstery vinyl: Use 54"-wide clear medium-weight upholstery vinyl to make the positioning overlay. You can usually find it in stores that carry upholstery fabric.

Clear heavyweight self-laminating sheets: Use these sheets to make templates. You can find them at most office supply stores and sometimes at warehouse markets. Buy the single-sided sheets, not the pouches. If you can't find the laminate, use clear Contac paper—it'll work in a pinch.

Sandpaper board: When tracing templates onto fabric, place the fabric on the sandpaper side of the board. Then place the template on the fabric. You'll love the way the sandpaper holds the fabric in place while you trace.

Wooden toothpick: Use a round toothpick to help turn under the turn-under allowance at points and curves. Wood has a texture that grabs and holds the fabric.

Fusible web: If you prefer to fuse and machine stitch the appliqué, use a paper-backed fusible web. Choose the one you like best and follow the directions on the package. It's a good idea to test the fusible web on the fabric you will be using.

Nonstick pressing sheet: If you are doing fusible appliqué, a nonstick pressing sheet will protect the iron and ironing board.

Full-spectrum work light: These lamps give off a bright and natural light. A floor lamp is particularly nice, as you can position it over your shoulder. Appliqué is so much easier when you can see what you are doing.

Batting: We prefer to use a cotton batt. Two of our favorites are Quilters Dream Cotton Batting and Hobbs Organic Cotton Batting.

Quilting gloves: Gloves make it easier to hold onto the quilt during machine quilting. We like the Machingers brand.

Sewing machine: Successful machine quilting requires the best sewing machine and table that you can afford. We love our Berninas!

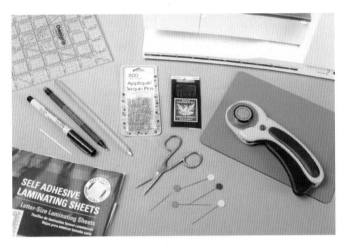

Appliqué supplies

Fabric Preparation

Prewash the fabric before using it. Prewashing is a good way not only to test for colorfastness, but to check shrinkage rates. Different fabrics shrink at different rates. It's better if the fabric shrinks **before** it is sewn into the quilt. Prewashed fabric has a better hand and it smells better. But the best reason to prewash is that it makes the fabric easier to hand appliqué.

About Our Fabric Requirements

Cotton fabric is usually 40″–44″ wide off the bolt. To be safe, we calculated all our fabric requirements based on a 40″ width.

Use the fabric requirements for each quilt as a guide, but remember that the yardage amounts will vary depending on how many fabrics you use and the sizes of the pieces you cut. Our measurements allow for both fabric shrinkage and a few errors in cutting.

Seam Allowances

All machine piecing is designed for ¼″ seam allowances.

Borders

The cutting instructions in this book are mathematically correct. However, variations in the finished size of the quilt top can result from slight differences in seam allowances. You should always measure **your** quilt before adding the borders. When measuring, be sure to measure the inside of the quilt top, not the outer edges that can stretch. Adjust the size of the borders if necessary.

Hand Appliqué or Fusible Web?

We prefer hand appliqué—you may not. Luckily we can each have it our own way. If you choose to use fusible web, please test the fabrics you plan to use. We recommend that you stitch around the outside of all fused appliqué pieces, either by hand or machine. Use a matching thread with solid fabrics for a more traditional look.

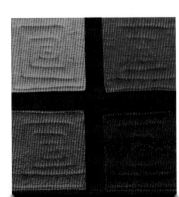

Color

Picture an Amish quilt in your mind. What is it about the fabric that you notice the most? It's solid. Solid fabric used in simple, traditional quilts is the signature of Amish quilts. These quilts feel bold. They often feel *contemporary*, which is a testament to their classic beauty.

The design of the quilt itself is very important when working with solids. Solid fabric has no pattern—the visual texture is smooth. The riot of color that comes with prints, plaids, and stripes is not there. When you use only solid fabric in a quilt, each shape is clearly defined. The structure of the pattern is there for all to see.

Building a Stash of Solids

It is interesting to limit your fabric palette to only solid fabrics—and it is certainly not what we are used to doing. Our fabric stashes are primarily made up of patterned fabrics, so we had to go out and find the solid fabrics for these quilts. We prefer hand-dyed solids. We could dye our own solids (and that is an option you have as well), but, honestly, that's just not where our interests lie. So we bought hand-dyed fabric where we could find it. We used solids off the bolt where we needed to.

When we were buying fabric we really didn't know how much we would need. We bought 2–4 yards of colors we thought we would use a lot of. We bought yardage in different shades of these colors as well. We bought lots of fat quarters of colors we thought we would use but weren't sure where. When it came time to make the quilts we often ran short of one fabric and had to substitute something else that may or may not have been close to the first fabric. This is good!

Part of the beauty of Amish quilts is that they aren't perfect. We're not talking about whether their seams match up perfectly; we're talking about the distribution of color in the quilt. If one fabric got used up, the quilt-maker switched to another piece of fabric. A quilt that is too perfect is just not as interesting as one that has a bit of color personality!

We worked out of our stashes of fabric. We couldn't easily get more of any one fabric. When we ran out of one fabric we were forced to switch to something else. Try it—it's lots of fun!

Color Theory

Color in quilts is always important. Color in Amish-style quilts takes on even greater importance because there are no patterns or prints. Some knowledge of the color wheel can help if you are not comfortable choosing colors. The *3-in-1 Color Tool* by Joen Wolfrom is helpful, as is the book *Color by Betty Edwards: A Course in Mastering the Art of Mixing Colors*. As you learn more about color theory, you'll understand that there are some color combinations that are just about foolproof. When you are unsure of your color choices, this is powerful information.

We're going to be honest: We don't think about color theory a lot. We understand the basics, and this is what works for us:

- We know that just about any colors can be used together.

- We know that the combination of values used (from light to dark) is what makes a pattern visible.

- We know that it is important to get everything up on the design wall *before* you start sewing! You can't guess at how colors are going to work together; you have to see it.

Inspiration

You can be inspired by just about anything: a picture in a book, a pretty carpet, the flowers outside your door—or another quilt. Becky saw an antique Amish quilt that looked very much like her *Triple Irish Chain*. The color combination was striking and the pattern was simple and bold. She made her own version for this book. *Lorna's Vine* grew out of that pieced quilt.

Regardless of where your inspiration comes from, you must first decide on the predominant color of your quilt. Every other color is built off this first choice. For example, Becky chose red as the predominant color for *Lorna's Vine*. It was an easy step to use greens for the vines and leaves because they are green in the real world. It just so happens that red and green are complementary colors, and boy, do they work well together!

Look again at *Lorna's Vine*. Where did the oranges, golds, and blues come from? These colors are next to the original choices of red and green on the color wheel—they are analogous colors. Becky didn't need to pull out a book or color tool, because the more you work with color, the more intuitive these choices become. If you don't have that intuition yet, or just want some guidance in certain situations, you **can** pull out the Color Tool.

Triple Irish Chain, made by Becky Goldsmith, 2005

3-in-1 Color Tool

Lorna's Vine, made by Becky Goldsmith, 2005

Linda chose a wonderful blue for the background of her *Baskets* quilt. The cool blues cried out to be warmed up with those luscious reds! Orange is the complement of blue—but Linda liked the red better. She relied on her eyes and experience; she put the red on the design wall with the blue and liked what she saw.

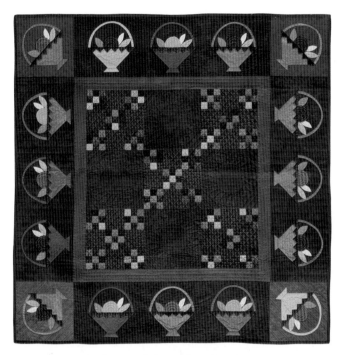

Baskets, made by Linda Jenkins, 2004

Making Decisions

Making decisions about the colors to use in *our* quilts is not as easy as you might imagine it to be. Even though we work intuitively with color, we work hard at selecting the color combinations that are just right. We spend as much time as it takes to get each fabric in our quilt right. A big quilt can take days to color. We aren't done until we're happy with what we see.

This is perhaps the most important thing we'd like to tell you about color. *You have to decide what you like.* You know more about color than you give yourself credit for.

You know what colors you like in clothes. You make color choices every day when you get dressed. You can't wear every color every day. You have to make specific choices for each outfit. You accessorize your outfits with jewelry, scarves, and pretty shoes. Imagine that those wonderful accessories are the accent colors in a quilt.

Combining colors well is not something that only *some* people can do. You can do it too. Believe in yourself! Refer to page 69 (Auditioning Your Fabric) for more on selecting fabrics.

Baskets

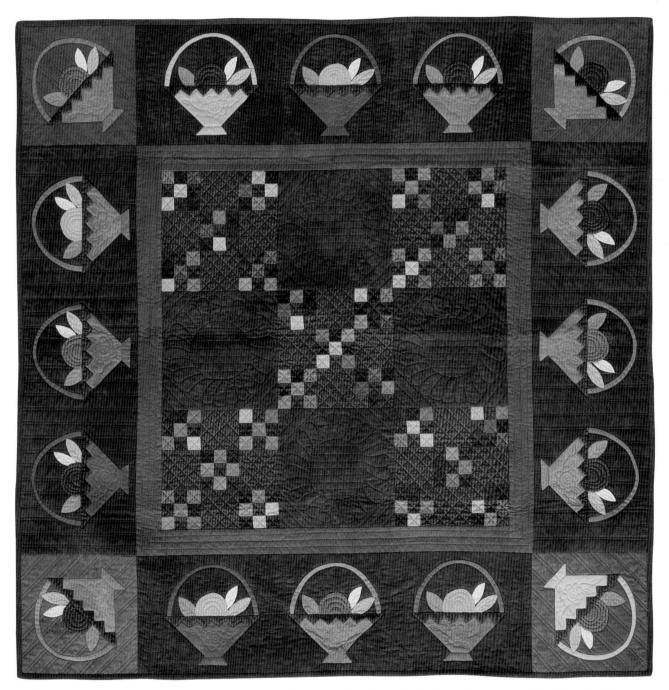

Made by Linda Jenkins, 2005

Finished quilt size: 49″ × 49″

Charming! Don't you think that is the best word for this quilt? The rich reds and golds are dazzling against the cool blues. What a treat for the eye.

Materials

This is a scrappy quilt. Use the yardage amounts below as a guide. They will vary with the number of fabrics you use.

Dark blue setting blocks and borders: 1⅔ yards

Medium blue inner border and border corners: 1 yard

Blue baskets and handles: A variety of fabrics to total 1½ yards

Bright red Nine-Patch setting blocks: ⅓ yard

Dark red Nine-Patch squares or strips: ¼ yard

Mixed color Nine-Patch fabrics: A variety of fabrics to total ¼ yard, including more reds for the baskets

Appliqué fabrics: A variety of large scraps of fabric

Binding: ⅞ yard

Backing and sleeve: 3¼ yards

Batting: 55″ × 55″

Cutting

Dark blue fabric

Setting blocks: Cut 4 squares 9½″ × 9½″.

Border: Cut 4 rectangles 11″ × 33½″.

Medium blue fabric

Inner border

    Top and bottom: Cut 2 strips 2½″ × 27½″.

    Sides: Cut 2 strips 2½″ × 31½″.

Border corners: Cut 4 squares 11″ × 11″.

Bright red fabric

Cut 20 squares 3½″ × 3½″.

Dark red fabric

*You can strip piece the Nine-Patches **or** make them from squares. Cut **either** strips **or** squares, not both.*

Cut 111 squares 1½″ × 1½″

OR cut 24 strips 1½″ × 8″.

Mixed color fabrics

*You can strip piece the Nine-Patches **or** make them from squares. Cut **either** strips **or** squares, not both.*

Cut 114 squares 1½″ × 1½″ in many colors

OR cut 24 strips 1½″ × 8″ in many colors.

    Binding

    Cut 1 square 26″ × 26″ to make a 2½″-wide continuous bias strip 240″ long. (Refer to page 74 for instructions.)

    Cut fabric for appliqué as needed.

Block Assembly

Be very careful to use an exact ¼″ seam allowance when piecing the blocks. If the Nine-Patch blocks grow or shrink, it will affect the way the blocks fit together.

You will make 25 Nine-Patch blocks for this quilt. The more traditional way to arrange the colors inside each block would be to have the mixed color squares arranged in an X.

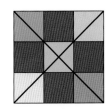

Colors arranged in an X

Linda wanted a very scrappy quilt. She made 14 blocks with the mixed colors arranged in the traditional way. She made 11 more blocks with the dark reds arranged in an X.

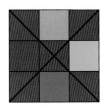

Dark reds arranged in an X

You have to look closely at the quilt to really see how the mixture of blocks and colors makes the quilt center so interesting.

1. If you cut 1½″ × 1½″ squares for your Nine-Patch blocks, arrange them on your design wall. Play with their placement until you are happy with it. To construct each block, sew the squares together into rows, then sew the rows together to make a square.

OR

If you prefer to strip piece the Nine-Patches, choose 16 strips 1½″ × 8″ from the mixed color fabrics. Sew a colorful strip to each side of a dark red strip. Don't plan which color goes where; just sew. Press toward the colorful strips. Make 8 colorful units.

Make 8 colorful units.

2. Cut 5 rows 1½″ wide from each unit for a total of 39 colorful pieced rows.

Cut 5 rows from each unit.

3. Choose 8 strips 1½″ × 8″ from the mixed color fabrics. Sew a red strip to each side of each colored strip. Make 8 red units.

Make 8 red units.

4. Cut 5 rows 1½″ wide from each unit, for a total of 36 pieced rows.

Cut 5 rows from each unit.

5. Sew 2 colorful rows to 1 red row. Make 14 colorful Nine-Patch blocks.

Make 14 colorful blocks.

6. Sew 2 red rows to 1 colorful row. Make 11 red Nine-Patch blocks.

7. Arrange the Nine-Patch blocks and bright red setting blocks on your wall. Play with their placement until you are happy. Then sew these blocks together into rows.

Sew blocks together into rows.

8. Sew the rows together into Double Nine-Patch blocks. Make 5.

Make 5 blocks.

Border Assembly

Refer to pages 64–69 for instructions on making the positioning overlay and preparing the appliqué. The appliqué pattern is on page 16.

There is one basket pattern for the border. Use it on the diagonal in the border corner blocks. Use it straight in the borders. Both diagonal and straight centerlines are marked on the pattern.

1. There are 3 baskets in each border strip. Note the spacing.

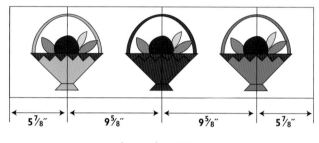

$5\frac{7}{8}''$ $9\frac{5}{8}''$ $9\frac{5}{8}''$ $5\frac{7}{8}''$

Border Appliqué Diagram

2. Make 3 copies of the border basket pattern. Draw a rectangle 9″ × 31″ on a strip of paper. Tape the basket patterns in place on the rectangle as indicated above.

3. Make templates and positioning overlays for the border and border corners from the paper patterns.

> **APPLIQUÉ TIPS**
> Use the *cutaway appliqué* technique to sew the basket handles, and use both the *cutaway* technique and *off-the-block construction* for the pointed trim on the basket. Refer to pages 71 and 72 for instructions.

4. Appliqué the borders and border corners.

5. Trim the border corners to $9\frac{1}{2}'' \times 9\frac{1}{2}''$.

6. Trim the borders to $9\frac{1}{2}'' \times 31\frac{1}{2}''$.

Quilt Assembly

Refer to the Quilt Assembly Diagram for quilt construction.

1. Arrange all the blocks on your design wall.

2. Sew the Nine-Patch and setting blocks together into rows. Press toward the setting blocks.

3. Sew the rows together. Press in the same direction.

4. Sew the top and bottom inner borders to the quilt. Press toward the inner border.

5. Sew the side inner borders to the quilt. Press toward the inner border.

6. Sew the side outer borders to the quilt. Press toward the inner border.

7. Sew a border corner block to each end of the remaining borders. Be sure to turn the corner blocks in the correct direction. Press toward the corner blocks.

8. Sew the top and bottom outer borders to the quilt. Press toward the inner border.

Quilting and Finishing

Refer to Quilting Techniques on pages 76–77. The quilting pattern is on the pullout at the back of the book. Refer to Finishing the Quilt on page 70 for layering, basting, and finishing.

1. Make a quilting stencil for the setting blocks. Place this stencil in the center of each setting block and lightly trace the design on it.

2. Use a rotary ruler to mark the grids on the quilt top.

3. Layer and baste the quilt. Quilt by hand or machine.

4. Finish the quilt.

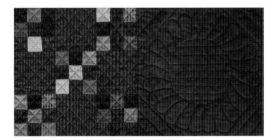

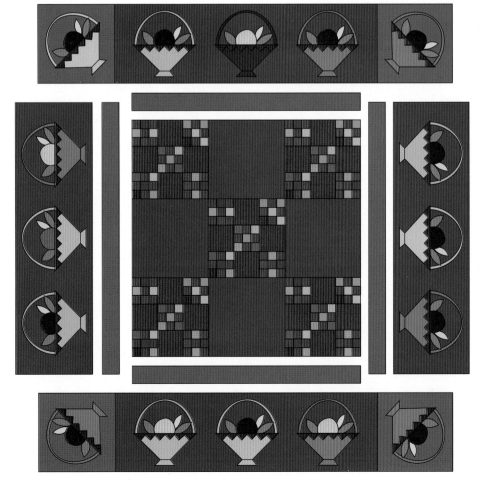

Quilt Assembly Diagram

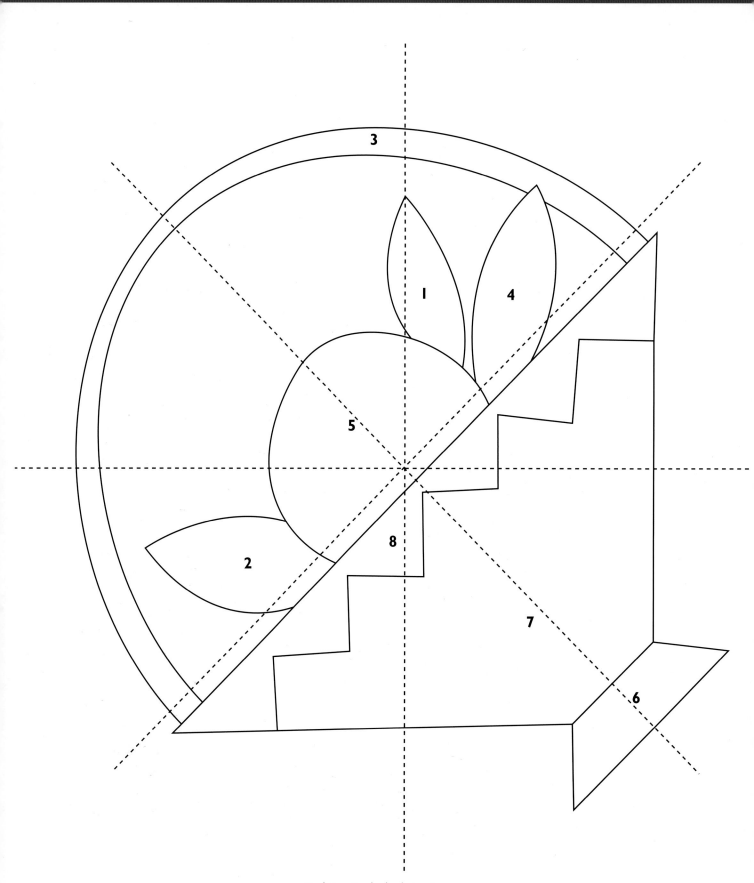

Baskets—Border basket pattern

Amish-Inspired Quilts

Lorna's Vine

Photo by Sharon Risedorph

Made by Becky Goldsmith, 2005

Finished quilt size: 71¼″ × 71¼″

Wow! This fiery red quilt demands to be looked at! Becky made it especially for her daughter-in-law, Lorna, who had a hand in the design of the quilt.

This quilt is inspired by the Triple Irish Chain *pattern (page 26)*. Initially Becky thought she would add appliqué to the open areas in that quilt. But when she did, the quilt became too crowded visually. Lorna said, "Why don't you put the appliqué where the piecing is?" What a perfect solution!

The criss-crossing vines mimic the piecing pattern in the Triple Irish Chain. The open spaces are preserved, leaving breathing space for the design. The quilted circular designs in the open spaces enhance the appliquéd feathered vines.

Materials

This quilt is scrappier than it looks. Becky pieced the backgrounds behind the vines and shaded them from dark at the base of the vine to light at the top. She also used multiple shades of green in the vines. Use the yardage amounts below as a guide. They will vary with the number of fabrics you use. If you run out of one fabric, piece in something similar.

Red appliqué background:

⅞ yard each of 4 shades of red for pieced blocks

OR 2¼ yards of red for solid blocks

Red background, setting blocks, border, and binding: 4 yards (You can use several reds as Becky did, or just one.)

Gold wheel appliqué backgrounds: A variety of fabrics to total 1⅛ yards

Green appliqué: A variety of fat quarters or large scraps of fabric to total approximately 2 yards

Green, red, orange, orange-red, and blue appliqué: A variety of fat quarters or large scraps of fabric (Becky used a variety of shades of each color.)

Backing and sleeve: 5 yards

Batting: 79″ × 79″

Cutting

Red fabrics

Becky pieced the backgrounds of her appliqué blocks. You can piece the backgrounds or not. If you piece the blocks, note the shading from dark to light. Cut **either** pieced **or** solid backgrounds, **not both**.

Pieced appliqué vine background

    A: Cut 36 strips 3¼″ × 8″.

    B: Cut 36 strips 2½″ × 8″.

    C: Cut 36 strips 2½″ × 8″.

    D: Cut 36 strips 3¼″ × 8″.

OR solid appliqué vine background

    Cut 36 rectangles 8″ × 10″.

Top and bottom borders: Cut 2 strips lengthwise 6½″ × 59¾″.

Side borders: Cut 2 strips lengthwise 6½″ × 71¾″.

Setting blocks

    Cut 13 squares 8½″ × 8½″.

    Cut 2 squares 12⅝″ × 12⅝″ for the side triangles; cut diagonally twice.

    Cut 2 squares 6⅜″ × 6⅜″ for the corner triangles; cut diagonally once.

Binding: Cut 1 square 29″ × 29″ to make a 2½″-wide continuous bias strip 320″ long. (Refer to page 74 for instructions.)

Gold fabric

Square appliqué backgrounds: Cut 12 squares 8″ × 8″.

Side triangle appliqué backgrounds: Cut 12 squares 12″ × 12″. **Do not cut the squares into triangles at this time.**

Cut fabric for appliqué as needed.

Block Assembly

Refer to pages 64–69 for instructions on making the positioning overlay and preparing the appliqué. The appliqué patterns are on the pullout at the back of the book.

APPLIQUÉ TIPS

Use the *cutaway appliqué* technique for the vine itself. Use *off-the block construction* for the wheel blocks, and use the *circle appliqué* technique for the center circles. Refer to pages 71 and 72 for instructions.

KEEPING TRACK OF YOUR BLOCKS

As we tell you on page 69, it is always a good idea to audition the background and appliqué fabrics on the design wall before you begin sewing. You may choose to make each vine block exactly the same and each wheel block exactly the same. In that case it won't matter where any individual block ends up in the quilt. However, if there are differences in the blocks, you will need to keep track of which block goes where.

Becky numbered her appliqué blocks so she knew where to put each block when the time came. Write the block number in a corner of the background at the edge, where it will be cut off when the block is trimmed.

Vine Blocks

1. If you are piecing the backgrounds for the vine blocks, do so now. Becky shaded the block backgrounds from dark at the bottom to light at the top.

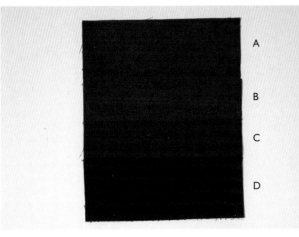

Piece the block backgrounds.

2. Appliqué the blocks. After the appliqué is complete, press the blocks on the wrong side.

3. Trim the blocks to 6½˝ × 8½˝. If you numbered the blocks for sewing, you will cut the number off at this point. Write the block number on a slip of paper and pin it to the block now.

Wheel Blocks—Center

1. The wheels are stitched off the block. Appliqué the spokes to the orange wheel fabric. (Becky used orange and orange-reds.) Stitch the center circle in place. Trim the wheel, leaving a ³⁄₁₆˝ seam allowance. Appliqué the completed wheel to the background.

2. After the appliqué is complete, press the blocks on the wrong side.

3. Trim the blocks to 6½˝ × 6½˝. If you numbered the blocks for sewing, you will cut the numbers off at this point. Write the block number on a slip of paper and pin it to the block now.

Wheel Blocks—Side

1. The backgrounds for the side blocks are cut square. The centering grid line on these blocks is on the **diagonal**. Press the blocks in half **diagonally**, creating a diagonal grid line.

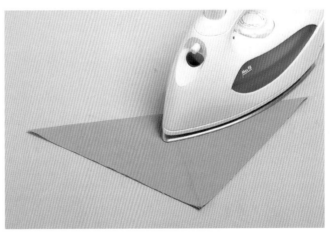

Press these backgrounds in half diagonally.

2. Appliqué the side wheel blocks. After the appliqué is complete, press the blocks on the wrong side.

3. Trim the blocks to 6½″ × 6½″.

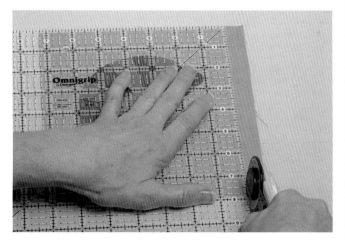

Trim the side blocks to 6½″ × 6½″.

4. Use a rotary ruler to measure ¼″ away from the long diagonal center of the block. Trim away the empty side of the block. If you numbered the blocks for sewing, you will cut the numbers off at this point. Write the block number on a slip of paper and pin it to the block now.

Add a ¼″ seam allowance to the diagonal and trim away the empty side of the block.

Quilt Assembly

Refer to the Quilt Assembly Diagram for quilt construction.

1. Arrange all the blocks on your design wall. Be sure that the vines are pointed in the proper direction.

2. Sew the blocks together in diagonal rows. Sew the lower left and upper right corners to the adjacent short rows. Press toward the setting blocks.

3. Sew the rows together. Press toward the rows with the setting blocks.

4. Sew the top and bottom borders to the quilt. Press toward the border.

5. Sew the side borders to the quilt. Press toward the border.

SIGNATURE BLOCK

We enjoy including our initials and the date on our quilts. This information is more personal when presented in your own handwriting. Place a piece of tracing paper over the vine block and draw your initials and the date, as Becky did on her quilt. Widen the letters and numbers until they are the size you want. Make templates and an overlay for your special appliquéd signature block.

Quilting and Finishing

Refer to Quilting Techniques on pages 76–77. The quilting patterns are on the pullout at the back of the book. Refer to Finishing the Quilt on page 70 for layering, basting, and finishing.

1. Make a quilting stencil for the border. Use this stencil to draw the quilt design on the quilt top. Space the border motifs evenly apart and centered within each border. Becky's designs are spaced 1⁷⁄₁₆″ apart.

2. Use a rotary ruler to mark the ¾″ grid lines on the quilt top.

3. Layer and baste the quilt. Quilt by hand or machine.

4. Finish the quilt.

Quilt Assembly Diagram

Feathers

Made by Linda Jenkins, 2005

Finished quilt size: 49½″ × 49½″

Feathers are a very common quilting motif in Amish quilts. Linda wondered what would happen if she appliquéd those lovely feathers—and here is the result. She used colors in her feathers that reminded her of a photograph of jewel-toned Amish clothes hanging in the breeze to dry. Her random placement of colors keeps your eye happily busy.

Materials

This is a scrappy quilt. Use the yardage amounts below as a guide. They will vary with the way you color the feathers.

Green setting triangles and borders: 2¼ yards

Deep fuchsia squares and feathers: ⅓ yard

Light blue squares and feathers: ⅓ yard

Dark blue block and inner borders, squares, and feathers: ¾ yard

Light green squares and feathers: ⅜ yard

Wine squares, bias stem vine, and feathers: ⅞ yard

Red squares and feathers: ⅜ yard

Purple squares and feathers: ⅓ yard

Binding: ⅞ yard

Backing and sleeve: 3⅓ yards

Batting: 58″ × 58″

Cutting

Green fabric

Setting triangles: Cut 2 squares 13⅝″ × 13⅝″; cut diagonally once.

Top and bottom borders: Cut 2 strips 12″ × 31½″.

Side borders: Cut 2 strips lengthwise 12″ × 51½″.

Deep fuchsia fabric

A: Cut 2 strips 1½″ × 40″, then cut 29 squares 1½″ × 1½″.

Light blue fabric

B: Cut 1 strip 1½″ × 40″, then cut 24 squares 1½″ × 1½″.

Dark blue fabric

Block border

    Short edge: Cut 2 strips 2″ × 15½″.

    Long edge: Cut 2 strips 2″ × 18½″.

Inner border

    Top and bottom: Cut 2 strips 2½″ × 26″.

    Sides: Cut 2 strips 2½″ × 30″.

Block squares

    C: Cut 2 strips 1½″ × 40″, then cut 36 squares 1½″ × 1½″.

Light green fabric

D: Cut 2 strips 1½″ × 40″, then cut 28 squares 1½″ × 1½″.

Wine fabric

Bias stem vine: Cut 1 square 22″ × 22″ to make a 1½″-wide continuous bias strip 300″ long. (Refer to page 73 for instructions.)

E: Cut 3 strips 1½″ × 40″, then cut 56 squares 1½″ × 1½″.

Red fabric

F: Cut 2 strips 1½″ × 40″, then cut 28 squares 1½″ × 1½″.

Purple fabric

G: Cut 1 strip 1½″ × 40″, then cut 24 squares 1½″ × 1½″.

Binding

Cut 1 square 26″ × 26″ to make a 2½″-wide continuous bias strip 240″ long. (Refer to page 74 for instructions.)

Cut fabric for appliqué as needed.

Block Assembly

There are ways to strip piece a Trip Around the World. However, we found that for a block this size it is easier to work with squares.

Be very careful to use an exact ¼″ seam allowance throughout this quilt. If the quilt grows or shrinks, it will affect the way the borders fit the quilt. If you find yourself in this predicament, adjust the size of the block borders.

1. Follow the Center Block Diagram and arrange the 1½″ × 1½″ squares on the wall.

2. Sew the squares together into rows. Press in alternate directions.

3. Sew the rows together to complete the block. Press in one direction.

4. Sew a short block border strip to the top and bottom of the block. Press toward the border.

5. Sew a long block border strip to each side of the block. Press toward the border.

6. The center block with borders attached should measure 18½″ × 18½″.

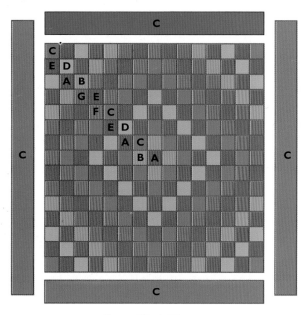

Center Block Diagram

Border Assembly

Refer to pages 64–69 for instructions on making the positioning overlay and preparing the appliqué. The appliqué patterns are on the pullout at the back of the book.

There are 2 patterns for the border: a straight border pattern and a corner border pattern. The top and bottom borders are short; the side borders are longer and contain the corners. There is a small part of each corner feather that is sewn down after the quilt is set together.

Border Appliqué Diagram

1. Make 4 copies of the straight border pattern.

2. Make 2 copies of the corner border pattern.

3. Tape 2 straight border patterns together to make a complete pattern for the top and bottom borders. Be careful to keep the centerlines straight. Extend each end of this short border paper pattern by 3″—this is where the feathers from the long borders will go.

4. Tape 2 straight border patterns and 2 corner border patterns together to make a complete pattern for the side borders. Be careful to keep the centerlines straight.

5. Make templates and overlays for both borders.

6. Make a ³⁄₁₆″-wide continuous bias stem for the vine (refer to page 73).

APPLIQUÉ TIPS

Feathers 1 and 2 are repeated throughout the border. In some places more of the feather may lie under the vine than in other places. Trim away excess fabric from the bases of these shorter feathers as necessary.

Appliqué the feathers in place, then position the bias vine. For pretty curves, pin the vine and then baste it in place, removing the pins as you baste.

7. Appliqué the borders. Remember to leave extra bias vine beyond the end of each corner. The rest of the vine is appliquéd after the quilt is set together. After the appliqué is complete, press the borders on the wrong side.

8. Trim the top and bottom borders to 10½˝ × 30˝.

9. Trim the side borders to 10½˝ × 50˝.

Quilt Assembly

Refer to the Quilt Assembly Diagram for quilt construction.

1. Sew a green setting triangle to each side of the center block. The long edge of the triangle is on the bias, so treat it gently. Press toward the block border.

2. Sew the top and bottom inner borders to the quilt. Press toward the inner border.

3. Sew the side inner borders to the quilt. Press toward the inner border.

4. Sew the top and bottom outer borders to the quilt. Press toward the inner border.

5. Sew the side outer borders to the quilt. Press toward the inner border.

6. Finish the appliqué in the border corners.

APPLIQUÉ TIP

Joining the bias vines can be a trick. It is easier if you very carefully trim some of the excess fabric from the underside at the ends of the vines. Cut one of the vines at an angle. Sew this angled vine end over the other end—turning under the raw edge as you normally would.

Quilting and Finishing

Refer to Quilting Techniques on pages 76–77. The quilting pattern is on the pullout at the back of the book. Refer to Finishing the Quilt on page 70 for layering, basting, and finishing.

1. Make a quilting stencil for the setting triangles. Place this stencil on the center of each setting triangle and lightly trace the design on it.

2. Use a rotary ruler to mark the straight quilting lines.

3. Layer and baste the quilt. Quilt by hand or machine.

4. Finish the quilt.

Quilt Assembly Diagram

Triple Irish Chain

Made by Becky Goldsmith, 2005

Finished quilt size: 49″ × 49″

This is a small version of an antique Amish quilt that Becky fell in love with. The colors practically vibrate! The Triple Irish Chain is a very traditional pattern, but these bold colors give the quilt a very modern attitude.

Materials

Red pieced blocks and border: $2\frac{1}{8}$ yards

Blue pieced blocks: 1 yard

Green pieced blocks: $\frac{2}{3}$ yard

Binding: $\frac{7}{8}$ yard

Backing and sleeve: 3 yards

Batting: $57'' \times 57''$

Cutting

Red fabric

Pieced blocks

    A: Cut 3 strips $1\frac{1}{2}'' \times 40''$.

    D: Cut 2 strips $3\frac{1}{2}'' \times 40''$.

    E: Cut 12 squares $5\frac{1}{2}'' \times 5\frac{1}{2}''$.

Borders

The border measurements listed here are mathematically correct. It is a good idea to wait to cut these until the blocks have been set together and you can measure your own quilt.

Cut 2 strips lengthwise $7\frac{1}{2}'' \times 49\frac{1}{2}''$.

Cut 2 strips $7\frac{1}{2}'' \times 35\frac{1}{2}''$.

Blue fabric

B: Cut 18 strips $1\frac{1}{2}'' \times 40''$.

Green fabric

C: Cut 13 strips $1\frac{1}{2}'' \times 40''$.

Binding

Cut 1 square $26'' \times 26''$ to make a $2\frac{1}{2}''$-wide continuous bias strip $240''$ long. (Refer to page 74 for instructions.)

Block Assembly

Be very careful to use an exact $\frac{1}{4}''$ seam allowance throughout this quilt. If the quilt grows or shrinks, it will affect the way the borders fit the quilt. If you find yourself in this predicament, adjust the size of the block borders and/or the inner borders.

1. Sew together 1 A strip, 4 B strips, and 2 C strips. Press in the direction of the arrow.

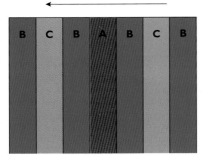

Sew strips together.

2. Cut 26 rows $1\frac{1}{2}''$ wide. Label these *Row 1*.

Cut 26 of Row 1.

3. Sew together 3 B strips and 4 C strips. Press in the direction of the arrow.

![Green and blue strips labeled C B C B C B C with arrow pointing right]

Sew strips together.

4. Cut 26 rows 1½″ wide. Label these *Row 2*.

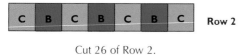

Cut 26 of Row 2.

5. Sew together 4 B strips and 3 C strips as shown below. Press in the direction of the arrow.

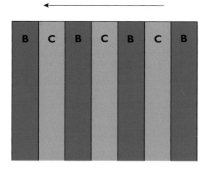

Sew strips together.

6. Cut 26 rows 1½″ wide. Label these *Row 3*.

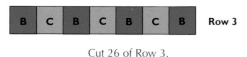

Cut 26 of Row 3.

7. Sew together 2 A strips, 3 B strips, and 2 C strips. Press in the direction of the arrow.

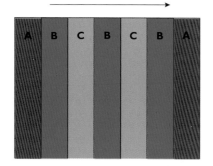

Sew strips together.

8. Cut 13 rows 1½″ wide. Label these *Row 4*.

Cut 13 of Row 4.

9. Sew rows 1–4 together to make Block 1. Be sure to alternate the pressed seams as indicated. Press the new seams in the direction of the arrow. Make 13 of Block 1.

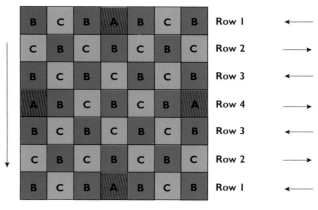

Make 13 of Block 1.

10. Sew together 2 B strips, 2 C strips, and 1 D strip. Press in the direction of the arrow.

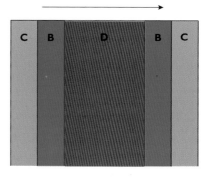

Sew strips together.

11. Cut 24 rows 1½″ wide. Label these *Row 5*.

Cut 24 of Row 5.

12. Sew together 2 B strips and 1 D strip. Press in the direction of the arrow.

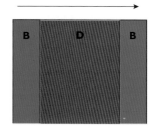

Sew strips together.

13. Cut 24 rows 1½″ wide. Label these *Row 6*.

Cut 24 of Row 6.

14. Sew 1 Row 6 to each side of the E square. Repeat for all E squares. Press in the direction of the arrow. Label these *Row 7*.

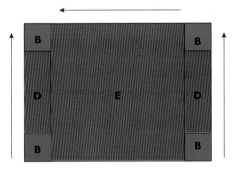

Sew Row 6 to each side of Square E.

15. Sew a Row 5 to the top and bottom of each Row 7 to make Block 2. Be sure to alternate the pressed seams as indicated. Press the new seams in the direction of the arrow. Make 12 of Block 2.

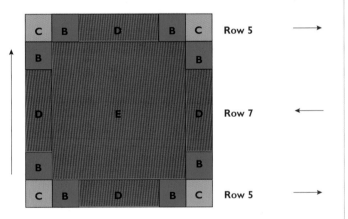

Make 12 of Block 2.

Quilt Assembly

Refer to the Quilt Assembly Diagram (page 30) for quilt construction.

1. Alternate the blocks as shown and sew them together into rows. Press the seams in alternate directions.

2. Sew the rows together to form the body of the quilt. Press the seams in the easiest direction.

3. Sew the side borders to the quilt. Press the seams toward the border.

4. Sew the top and bottom borders to the quilt. Press the seams toward the border.

Quilting and Finishing

Refer to Quilting Techniques on pages 76–77. The quilting patterns are the pullout at the back of the book. Refer to Finishing the Quilt on page 70 for layering, basting, and finishing.

1. Make a quilting stencil for the setting blocks. Becky used the quilting pattern from the border of *Lorna's Vine*. Use this stencil to draw the quilt designs on the quilt top. Be sure to center the design on the setting blocks.

2. Becky drew a freehand feathered border directly onto her quilt. If you haven't done this before, practice drawing feathers on paper first.

3. Layer and baste the quilt. Quilt by hand or machine.

4. Finish the quilt.

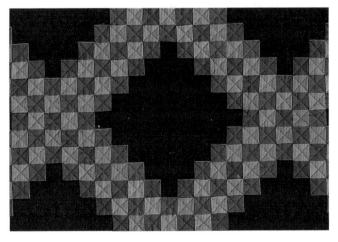

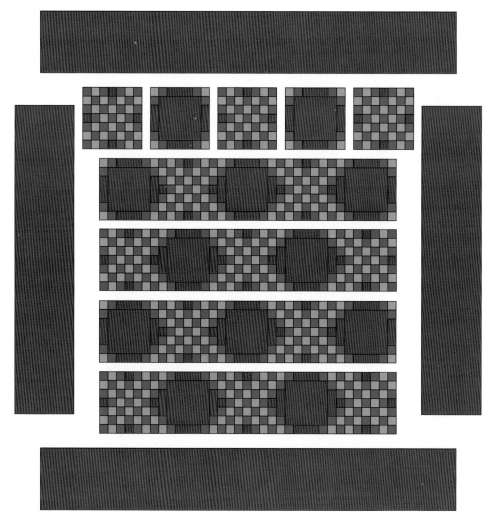

Quilt Assembly Diagram

Amish-Inspired Quilts

Birds of a Feather

Made by Becky Goldsmith, 2005

Finished quilt size: 67″ × 73″

Amish bar quilts are elegant in their simplicity. Becky decided to work within the bounds of that traditional simplicity. She chose to appliqué the Flying Geese, layering triangles of different value and color. There are no center seams in the birds, resulting in a softer appearance.

As you can see, Becky ran out of the primary fabrics she was using for the gold sashing, the green bars, and the blue border. She used the next best fabric that she had on hand. Rather than detracting from the quilt, these new fabrics add a spark of character.

Materials

This is a scrappy quilt. Use the yardage amounts below as a guide. They will vary with the number of fabrics you use. If you run out of one fabric, piece in something similar.

Blue appliqué background: A variety of fabrics to total 2¼ yards

Blue border: 3½ yards

Green vertical bars and largest triangles: A variety of fabrics to total 3 yards

Yellow-green medium triangles: A variety of fabrics to total 1½ yards

Gold sashing and small triangles: A variety of fabrics to total 1 yard

Binding: 1 yard

Backing and sleeve: 5 yards

Batting: 75″ × 81″

Cutting

Note: The Flying Geese are stitched using off-the-block construction. Refer to pages 72–73 **before** cutting the Flying Geese triangles.

Blue fabrics

Appliqué backgrounds: Cut 68 rectangles 5″ × 8″.

Side borders: Cut 2 strips lengthwise 10½″ × 53½″.

Top and bottom borders: Cut 2 strips lengthwise 10½″ × 67½″.

Green fabrics

Wide vertical bars: Cut 4 strips 5½″ × 40″; construct 3 strips 5½″ × 51½″.

Large Flying Geese: Cut 68 using Template 1.

Yellow-green fabrics

Cut 68 using Template 2.

Gold fabrics

Vertical sashing: Cut 11 strips 1½″ × 40″; construct 8 strips 1½″ × 51½″.

Top and bottom sashing: Cut 3 strips 1½″ × 40″; construct 2 strips 1½″ × 47½″.

Small geese: Cut 68 using Template 3.

Binding

Cut 1 square 29″ × 29″ to make a 2½″-wide continuous bias strip 320″ long. (Refer to page 74 for instructions.)

Block Assembly

Refer to pages 64–69 for instructions on making the positioning overlay and preparing the appliqué. The appliqué pattern is on page 34.

APPLIQUÉ TIP
Use *off-the-block construction* for the Flying Geese. Refer to pages 72–73 for instructions.

KEEPING TRACK OF YOUR BLOCKS
As we tell you on page 69, it is always a good idea to audition the background and appliqué fabrics on the design wall before you begin sewing. You may choose to make each bird block exactly the same. In that case it won't matter where any individual block ends up in the quilt. However, if there are differences in the blocks, you will need to keep track of which block goes where.

Number the appliqué blocks from top to bottom by column so you know where to put each block when the time comes. Write the block number in a corner of the background at the edge, where it will be cut off when the block is trimmed.

1. The birds are stitched off the block—appliqué the triangles from the top down.

2. After the 3 triangles are stitched together, trim the fabric behind each shape, leaving a ³⁄₁₆″ seam allowance. Appliqué the completed bird to the background.

3. After the appliqué is complete, press the blocks on the wrong side.

4. Trim the blocks to 3½″ × 6½″. If you numbered the blocks for sewing, you will cut the numbers off at this point. Write the block number on a slip of paper and pin it to the block now.

Quilt Assembly

Refer to the Quilt Assembly Diagram (page34) for quilt construction.

1. Arrange all the blocks on your design wall.

2. Sew the bird blocks together into vertical rows. Press in the easiest direction.

3. Sew a vertical sashing strip to each side of the bird bars. Press toward the sashing.

4. Sew the green vertical bars between the bird bars as shown. Press toward the sashing.

5. Sew the top and bottom sashing strips to the quilt. Press toward the sashing.

6. Sew the side borders to the quilt. Press toward the sashing.

7. Sew the top and bottom borders to the quilt. Press toward the sashing.

Quilting and Finishing

Refer to Quilting Techniques on pages 76–77. Refer to Finishing the Quilt on page 70 for layering, basting, and finishing.

1. All seams are quilted in the ditch.

2. Use a rotary ruler to draw straight grid lines spaced ³⁄₄″ apart in the green vertical bars.

3. Fill the bird blocks with free-motion feathers and zigzags.

4. Fill the sashing with 3 lines of channel quilting.

5. Alternate lines of ½″ channel quilting with 2″-wide strips of free-motion feathers in the borders.

6. Layer and baste the quilt. Quilt by hand or machine.

7. Finish the quilt.

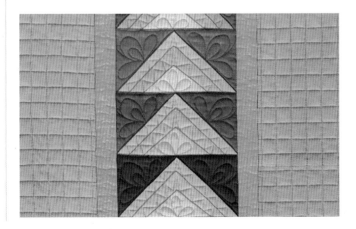

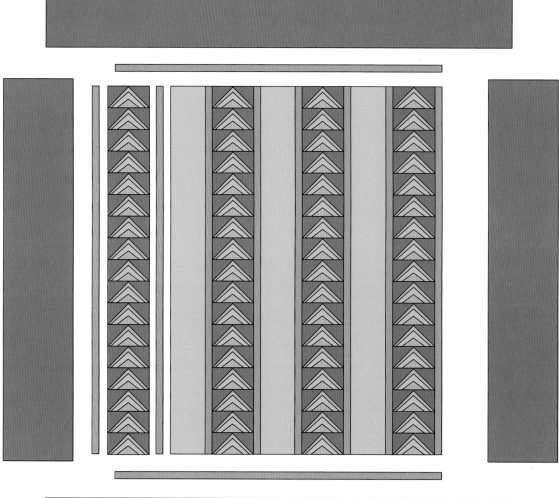

Quilt Assembly Diagram

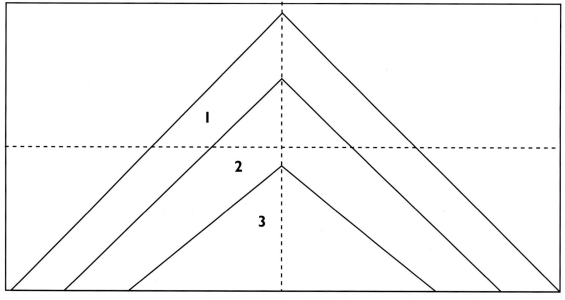

Birds of a Feather—Bird block

  Amish-Inspired Quilts

Quilt Fragments

Some old quilts have been loved and used so much that only bits of them are left. These leftover bits may be only a fraction of what the whole quilt once was, but many are quite interesting standing alone. We call them "quilt fragments." A photograph of a portion of a quilt is also a kind of quilt fragment. We liked the idea of fragments so much that we decided to design some for this book.

Quilt fragments are a lot of fun to work on. They are small quilts and are fast to make—they aren't as intimidating as a big quilt. We treated ours as quilt studies, playing with different design ideas. These ideas may grow into something bigger later—or not. The important thing is what we learned as we designed each one.

If you haven't worked on quilts in a series before, this is a good place to try it. You can make the same fragment in a variety of different colors and fabrics. You can make several of the fragments from related colors and fabrics. Play with paint, embellishments, new machine stitching—whatever is interesting to you. Have fun!

From Becky

My son Jeff is hard to make a quilt for. He likes the quilts I make, but he has never really wanted one. It sort of hurt my feelings, but like a good mother, I just kept on offering them, figuring that one day he'd want a quilt.

Well, that day finally arrived. He was home from college when he saw the four fragments that I was working on and he immediately claimed them! Boy, was I surprised. He said he didn't like weird colors—which must mean that the greens and golds I used look *unusual*, not weird.

Jeff said these quilts didn't look like me. Because I love him, I chose to overlook the fact that he especially likes these quilts that don't "look like me." I tend to like symmetry, floral motifs, and lots of patterned fabric. These fragments are asymmetrical, not floral, and made from bold solid fabrics. They're me on the inside.

Jeff is a math major. He studied the quilts I was working on, and after a while announced that they represented the numbers 7, 8, 9, and 10. I've decided that he looks for different things in quilts than I do, but if it makes him happy, that's just fine too.

Squares & Rectangles

Made by Becky Goldsmith, 2005

Finished quilt size: 18″ × 24″

The title says squares and rectangles but it can be hard to find the rectangles. They hide at the bottom of the quilt— the purples blending into the background.

Materials

This is a scrappy quilt. Because it is small, it doesn't take much of any one fabric. Use the yardage amounts below as a guide. They will vary with the number of fabrics you use.

Purple background blocks and borders: ⅞ yard

Green sashing: ⅛ yard

Appliqué fabrics: A variety of scraps of fabric

Binding: ⅔ yard

Backing and sleeve: ¾ yard

Batting: 24″ × 30″

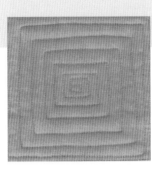

Cutting

Refer to page 39 for color letter references.

Purple fabric

A: Cut 1 strip 11″ × 24″.

B: Cut 1 strip 7½″ × 24″.

C: Cut 2 strips 1½″ × 22½″.

D: Cut 2 strips 1½″ × 18½″.

Green fabric

E: Cut 3 strips 1″ × 22½″.

Binding

Cut 1 square 19″ × 19″ to make a 2½″-wide continuous bias strip 125″ long. (Refer to page 74 for instructions.)

Cut fabric for appliqué as needed.

Block Assembly

Refer to pages 64–69 for instructions on making the positioning overlay and preparing the appliqué. The appliqué patterns are on page 39.

Block A

1. Make templates for Square 1 and Rectangle 2.

2. Draw a rectangle 9″ × 22″ on a piece of paper. Draw a line 1″ in from each of the long sides. Draw a line 1¼″ in from each of the short sides.

3. Draw a center horizontal and vertical line.

4. Trace around templates 1 and 2. It's okay if the spacing isn't *perfect*. That will add to the charm.

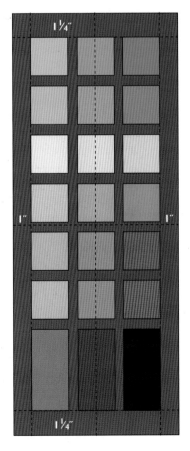

Block A

5. Make the positioning overlay from the paper pattern.

6. Appliqué Block A with pieces cut from Templates 1 and 2.

7. After the appliqué is complete, press the block on the wrong side.

8. Trim the block to 9½″ × 22½″.

Block B

1. Make a template from Square 3.

2. Draw a rectangle 5½″ × 22″ on a piece of paper. Draw a line ¾″ in from each of the long sides. Draw a line 1¼″ in from each of the short sides.

3. Draw a center horizontal and vertical line.

4. Draw around template 3. It's okay if the spacing isn't *perfect*.

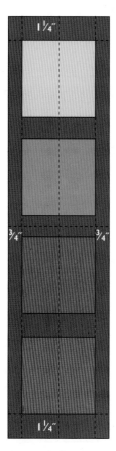

Block B

5. Make the overlay from the paper pattern.

6. Appliqué Block B using pieces cut from Template 3.

7. After the appliqué is complete, press the block on the wrong side.

8. Trim the block to 6″ × 22½″.

Quilt Assembly

Refer to the Quilt Assembly Diagram for quilt construction.

1. Arrange blocks A and B and strips C and E on your design wall.

2. Sew the blocks and strips together. Press toward the purple.

3. Sew an E strip to the top and bottom of the quilt. Press toward the E strips.

Quilting and Finishing

Refer to Quilting Techniques on pages 76–77. Refer to Finishing the Quilt on page 70 for layering, basting, and finishing.

1. You can mark quilting designs on the quilt top or plan to stitch without marking.

2. Layer and baste the quilt. Quilt by hand or machine.

3. Finish the quilt.

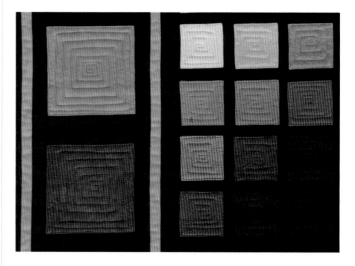

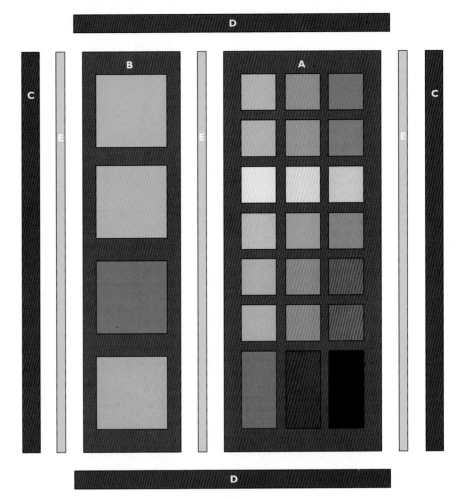

Quilt Assembly Diagram

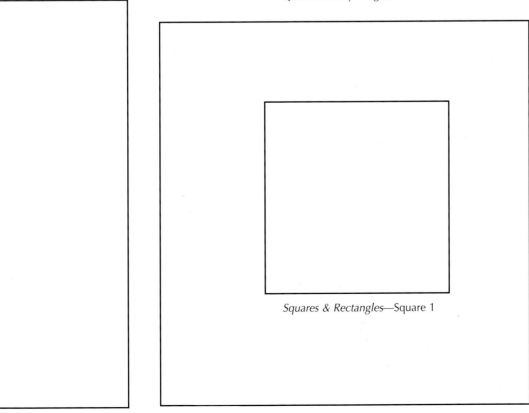

Squares & Rectangles—Rectangle 2

Squares & Rectangles—Square 1

Squares & Rectangles—Square 3

Eight Birds

Made by Becky Goldsmith, 2005

Finished quilt size: 18″ × 24″

You can easily imagine that this is a fragment from a bar quilt. Experiment with fabric on your design wall until the composition appears balanced.

Materials

This is a scrappy quilt. Because it is small, it doesn't take much of any one fabric. Use the yardage amounts below as a guide. They will vary with the number of fabrics you use.

Green bar: ¼ yard

Green-gold bar: ¼ yard

Gold appliqué background: ⅓ yard

Purple bars: ⅛ yard

Appliqué fabrics: A variety of scraps of fabric

Binding: ⅔ yard

Backing and sleeve: ¾ yard

Batting: 24″ × 30″

Cutting

Green fabric

Cut 1 strip 6½″ × 24½″.

Green-gold fabric

Cut 1 strip 4″ × 24½″.

Gold fabric

Cut 8 strips 5″ × 8″.

Purple fabric

A: Cut 2 strips 1½″ × 24½″.

B: Cut 1 strip 1″ × 24½″.

Binding

Cut 1 square 19″ × 19″ to make a 2½″-wide continuous bias strip 125″ long. (Refer to page 74 for instructions.)

Cut fabric for appliqué as needed.

Block Assembly

Refer to pages 64–69 for instructions on making the positioning overlay and preparing the appliqué. Use the Birds of a Feather appliqué pattern on page 34.

> **APPLIQUÉ TIP**
>
> Use *off-the-block construction* for the birds (Flying Geese). Refer to pages 72–73 for instructions.

1. Make the templates and positioning overlay.

2. The birds are stitched off the block—appliqué the triangles from the top down. Make 8 birds.

3. After the 3 triangles are stitched together, trim the fabric behind each shape, leaving a ³⁄₁₆″ seam allowance. Appliqué the completed bird to the background. Make 8 blocks.

4. After the appliqué is complete, press the blocks on the wrong side.

5. Trim the blocks to 3½″ × 6½″.

Quilt Assembly

Refer to the Quilt Assembly Diagram (page 42) for quilt construction.

1. Arrange all the blocks and bars on your design wall.

2. Sew the blocks together into a bar. Press in the easiest direction.

3. Sew the bars together. Press toward the purple strips.

Quilting and Finishing

Refer to Quilting Techniques on pages 76–77. Refer to Finishing the Quilt on page 70 for layering, basting, and finishing.

1. You can mark quilting designs on the quilt top or plan to stitch without marking.

2. Layer and baste the quilt. Quilt by hand or machine.

3. Finish the quilt.

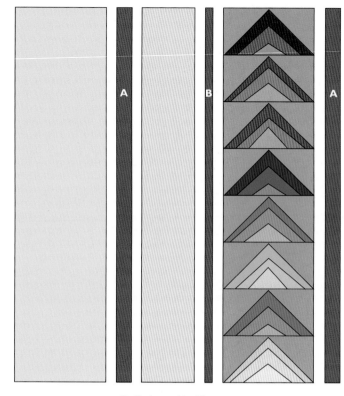

Quilt Assembly Diagram

Vine #9

Made by Becky Goldsmith, 2005

Finished quilt size: 18″ × 24″

Becky used the vine block from Lorna's Vine *as the centerpiece for this fragment. The nine leaves in the vine give this piece its name.*

Materials

This is a scrappy quilt. Because it is small, it doesn't take much of any one fabric. Use the yardage amounts below as a guide. They will vary with the number of fabrics you use.

Purple appliqué background and borders: A variety of fabrics to total ⅝ yard

Blue border: A variety of fabrics to total ⅛ yard

Green borders: A variety of fabrics to total ¼ yard

Gold border: ⅛ yard

Appliqué fabrics: A variety of scraps of fabric to total about ¼ yard

Binding: ⅔ yard

Backing and sleeve: ¾ yard

Batting: 24″ × 30″

Cutting

Refer to page 45 for color number reference.

Purple fabric

Appliqué background: Cut 1 strip 8″ × 10″.

Borders:

9: Cut assorted pieces 3″ wide; construct 1 strip 3″ × 15½″.

10: Cut assorted pieces 3½″ wide; construct 1 strip 3½″ × 16″.

11: Cut 1 strip 4″ × 18½″.

12: Cut 1 strip 5½″ × 18½″.

Blue fabrics

These strips are constructed with small bits of fabric in the appropriate color.

1: Cut assorted pieces 1½″ wide; construct 2 strips 1½″ × 8½″.

2: Cut assorted pieces 1½″ wide; construct 2 strips 1½″ × 8½″.

Green fabrics

These strips are constructed with small bits of fabric in the appropriate color.

3: Cut assorted pieces 2½″ wide; construct 1 strip 2½″ × 10½″.

4: Cut assorted pieces 2½″ wide; construct 1 strip 2½″ × 10½″.

5: Cut assorted pieces 1½″ wide; construct 1 strip 1½″ × 12½″.

6: Cut assorted pieces 1½″ wide; construct 1 strip 1½″ × 11½″.

7: Cut 1 strip 2″ × 13½″.

Gold fabric

8: Cut 1 strip 3″ × 13″.

Binding

Cut 1 square 19″ × 19″ to make a 2½″-wide continuous bias strip 125″ long. (Refer to page 74 for instructions.)

Cut fabric for appliqué as needed.

Block Assembly

Refer to pages 64–69 for instructions on making the positioning overlay and preparing the appliqué. Use the Lorna's Vine appliqué pattern on the pullout at the back of the book.

> **APPLIQUÉ TIP**
> Use the *cutaway appliqué* technique for the vine itself. Refer to page 71 for instructions.

1. Make the templates and the positioning overlay.

2. Appliqué the block.

3. After the appliqué is complete, press the block on the wrong side.

4. Trim the block to 6½″ × 8½″.

Quilt Assembly

Refer to the Quilt Assembly Diagram for quilt construction.

1. Arrange the vine block and strips 1–12 on your design wall.

2. Sew a Strip 1 to each side of the block. Press toward the border.

3. Sew a Strip 2 to the top and bottom of the block. Press toward the border.

4. Continue sewing on the strips in numerical order, pressing toward the border.

Quilting and Finishing

Refer to Quilting Techniques on pages 76–77. Refer to Finishing the Quilt on page 70 for layering, basting, and finishing.

1. You can mark quilting designs on the quilt top or plan to stitch without marking.

2. Layer and baste the quilt. Quilt by hand or machine.

3. Finish the quilt.

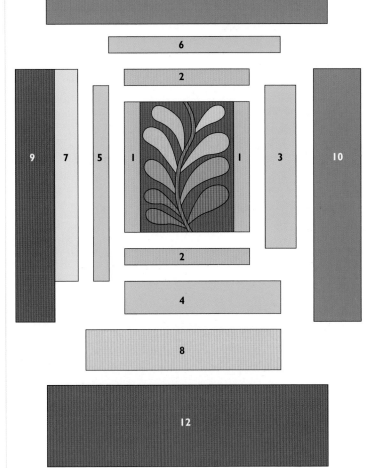

Quilt Assembly Diagram

Crazy #10

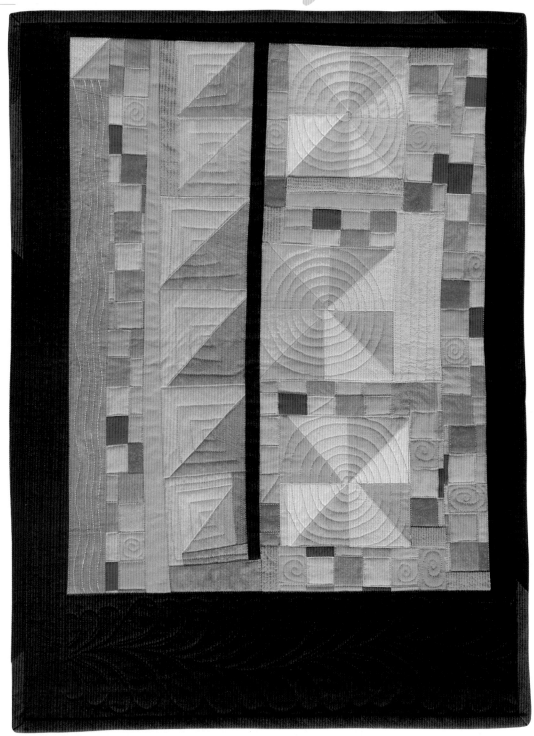

Made by Becky Goldsmith, 2005

Finished quilt size: 18″ × 24″

There is a reason that we call this a crazy quilt. There is no plan, no pattern. For those of us used to having a plan, this is hard work, and it feels crazy. But here's a fact: It is good for your brain to try something different every now and then. The 18″ × 24″ format is a great place to start.

There is no pattern. We can't be very specific about yardage or cutting or construction. What we can do is offer guidelines for you to use when you make your crazy quilt.

Go crazy every now and then.

(FYI: Becky's son Jeff decided that this quilt is #10. There are 3 Pinwheel blocks and 7 plain triangle-square blocks: 3 + 7 = 10. Being able to hang 7, 8, 9, and 10 together makes him happy—mathematicians are so funny!)

Materials

Any leftover blocks, strips, or bits of fabric are fair game. Use what you have.

Binding: ⅔ yard

Backing and sleeve: ¾ yard

Batting: 24″ × 30″

Cutting

Binding

Cut 1 square 19″ × 19″ to make a 2½″-wide continuous bias strip 125″ long (refer to page 74 for instructions).

OR consider using leftover strips of binding from other quilts.

Guidelines

1. Use the fabric you have. It will force you to be more creative.

2. Put away the rotary ruler and cutter. Find your good shears. This is hard, but necessary. Crazy quilts have a loose, fluid line quality that is decidedly different from the hard edges that come from rotary tools.

3. Keep the color scheme simple if you are new to this.

4. Keep the design elements simple—squares, triangle-squares, rectangles.

5. If you are using leftover blocks, don't be afraid to cut them up. Use the shears and make cuts in off places—not along seamlines.

6. We are used to working with 90° and 45° angles—try to soften them up. Make the cuts slightly askew.

7. Use coping strips to make units fit together. The hot pink vertical strip next to the top 2 triangle-squares on the left side of the quilt is a coping strip. It helps the 2 triangle-squares fit in the row.

8. Work on your design wall. Move elements around. Take digital pictures of different versions to help you remember what you have tried.

CRAZY TIPS

Making a crazy quilt takes longer than you think it will. Becky spent the better part of two days getting her quilt just the way she wanted it.

She was working with blocks of squares that she had left over from another project. She really thought that these blocks would be the primary design element. Instead she found that they were better cut up and used in a secondary role. Even when you have a plan in mind, be willing to change it if it isn't working.

Quilt Assembly

1. Sew the top together.

Quilting and Finishing

Refer to Quilting Techniques on pages 76–77. Refer to Finishing the Quilt on page 70 for layering, basting, and finishing.

1. You can mark quilting designs on the quilt top or plan to stitch without marking.

2. Layer and baste the quilt. Quilt by hand or machine.

3. Finish the quilt.

Nine-Patch Fragment

Made by Linda Jenkins, 2005

Finished quilt size: 18˝ × 24˝

Linda used an unusual combination of colors to make this stunning piece. The greens add a cool touch to the hot oranges and purples.

Materials

This is a scrappy quilt. Use the yardage amounts below as a guide. They will vary with the number of fabrics you use.

Orange Nine-Patch setting blocks and small squares: A variety of fabrics to total ⅜ yard

Green small squares and narrow strip: A variety of fabrics to total ¼ yard

Purple setting triangles and wide strip: ⅝ yard

Binding: ⅔ yard

Backing and sleeve: ¾ yard

Batting: 24″ × 30″

Cutting

Orange fabrics

Setting blocks: Cut 12 squares 3½″ × 3½″.

Small squares: Cut 74 squares 1½″ × 1½″.

Green fabrics

Small squares: Cut 89 squares 1½″ × 1½″.

Narrow strip: Cut 1 strip 1″ × 28″.

Purple fabric

Setting triangles: Cut 1 square 14″ × 14″, cut diagonally twice.

Wide strip: Cut 1 strip 6″ × 28″.

Binding

Cut 1 square 19″ × 19″ to make a 2½″-wide continuous bias strip 125″ long. (Refer to page 74 for instructions.)

Block Assembly

1. Arrange the setting squares and small light and dark squares on your design wall to form 3 Double Nine-Patch blocks.

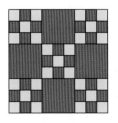

Double Nine-Patch Diagram

2. Sew the Double Nine-Patch blocks together. Press the seams in alternate directions. Make 3 blocks.

Make 3 blocks.

3. Sew the remaining small squares together into a strip.

Quilt Assembly

1. Arrange all the blocks and bars on your design wall.

2. Sew the triangles to the Double Nine-Patch blocks. Press toward the triangles.

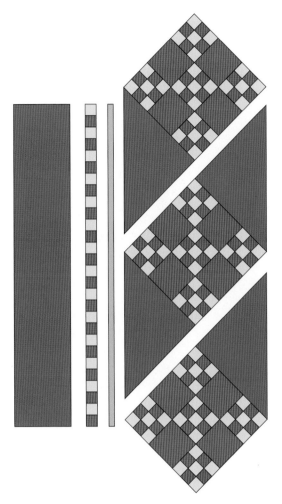

Sew triangles to Double Nine-Patch blocks.

3. Sew the diagonal rows together. Press toward the bottom of the quilt.

4. Sew the wide strip to the left side of the strip of squares. Press toward the wide strip.

5. Sew the narrow strip to the right side of the strip of squares. Press toward the narrow strip.

6. Sew the 2 sides of the quilt together. Press toward the narrow strip.

7. Trim the quilt to 18½″ × 24½″.

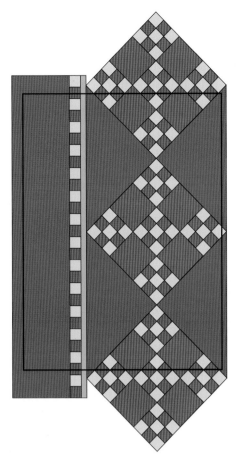

Trim quilt to size.

Quilting and Finishing

Refer to Quilting Techniques on pages 76–77. Refer to Finishing the Quilt on page 70 for layering, basting, and finishing.

1. You can mark quilting designs on the quilt top or plan to stitch without marking.

2. Layer and baste the quilt. Quilt by hand or machine.

3. Finish the quilt.

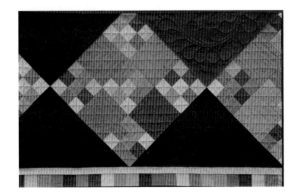

Circles
Fragment

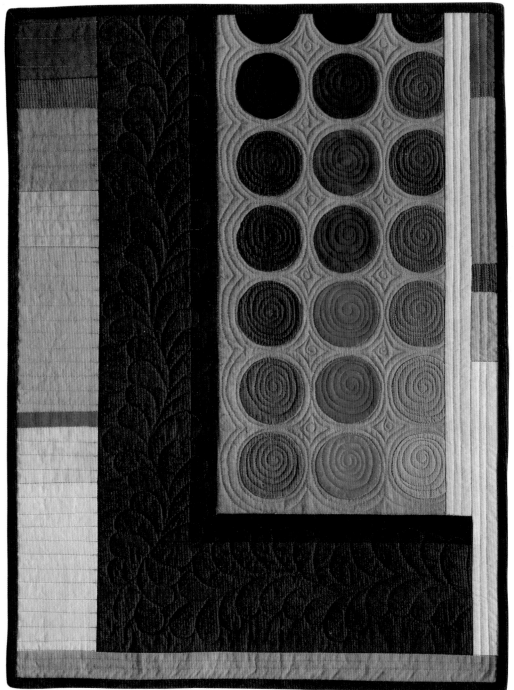

Made by Linda Jenkins, 2005

Finished quilt size: 18˝ × 24˝

Linda's circles are so elegantly stacked. One little jiggle and you expect them to roll onto the floor like gumballs!

Materials

This is a scrappy quilt. Because it is small, it doesn't take much of any one fabric. Use the yardage amounts below as a guide. They will vary with the number of fabrics you use.

Green appliqué background and borders: A variety of fabrics to total ⅝ yard

Dark purple inner border: ⅛ yard

Purple outer border: ¼ yard

Appliqué fabrics: A variety of scraps of fabric to total about ¼ yard

Binding: ⅔ yard

Backing and sleeve: ¾ yard

Batting: 24″ × 30″

Cutting

Refer to page 55 for color number references.

Green fabric

Appliqué background: Cut 1 strip 10½″ × 20″.

Borders:

    2: Cut 1 strip 1½″ × 18½″.

    7: Cut assorted pieces 3½″ wide; construct 1 strip 3½″ × 23½″. Include color accents.

    8: Cut assorted pieces 1½″ wide; construct 1 strip 1½″ × 23½″. Include color accents.

    9: Cut 1 strip 1½″ × 18½″.

Dark purple fabric

3: Cut 1 strip 1½″ × 10″.

4: Cut 1 strip 1½″ × 19½″.

Purple fabric

5: Cut 1 strip 4″ × 19½″.

6: Cut 1 strip 4½″ × 14½″.

Binding

Cut 1 square 19″ × 19″ to make a 2½″-wide continuous bias strip 125″ long. (Refer to page 74 for instructions.)

Cut fabric for appliqué as needed.

Block Assembly

Refer to pages 64–69 for instructions on making the positioning overlay and preparing the appliqué. The appliqué pattern is on page 54.

1. Make the circle template.

2. Draw a rectangle 8½″ × 18″ on a piece of paper. Draw a center horizontal and vertical line.

3. Draw a line ¾″ in from the long left side. Draw a line ⅜″ up from the short bottom side.

4. Draw circles on the rectangle by tracing around the template. It's okay if the spacing isn't *perfect*. That will add to the charm. Notice that the circles along the top and right side are cut off.

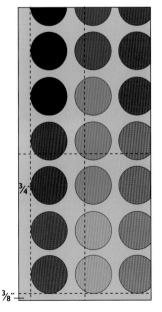

Block Diagram

5. Make the overlay from the paper pattern.

6. Appliqué the circles onto the green background.

7. After the appliqué is complete, press the block on the wrong side.

8. Trim the block to 9″ × 18½″.

Quilt Assembly

Refer to the Quilt Assembly Diagram for quilt construction.

1. Arrange the circle block and Strips 1–9 on your design wall.

2. Sew Strip 2 to the right side of the block. Press toward the border.

3. Sew Strip 3 to the bottom of the block. Press toward the border.

4. Sew Strip 4 to the left side of the block. Press toward the border.

5. Sew Strip 5 to the left side of the block. Press toward the border.

6. Sew Strip 6 to the bottom of the block. Press toward the border.

7. Sew Strip 7 to the left side of the block. Press toward the border.

8. Sew Strip 8 to the right side of the block. Press toward the border.

9. Sew Strip 9 to the bottom of the block. Press toward the border.

Quilting and Finishing

Refer to Quilting Techniques on pages 76–77. Refer to Finishing the Quilt on page 70 for layering, basting, and finishing.

1. You can mark quilting designs on the quilt top or plan to stitch without marking.

2. Layer and baste the quilt. Quilt by hand or machine.

3. Finish the quilt.

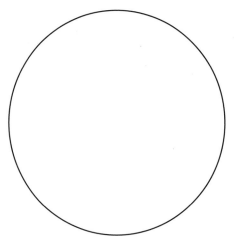

Circles Fragment—Circle

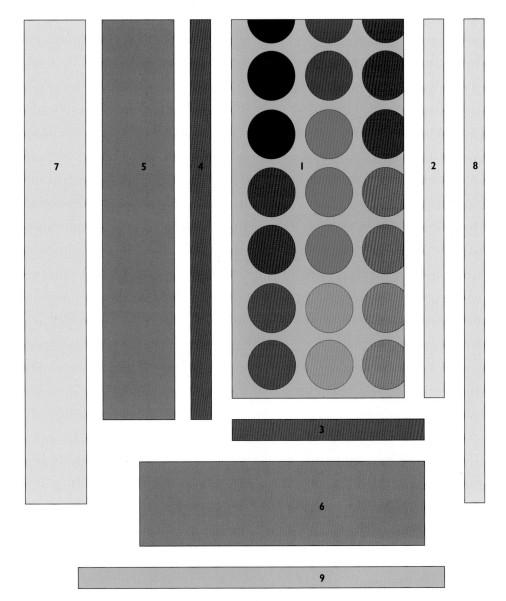

Quilt Assembly Diagram

Basket
Fragment

Made by Linda Jenkins, 2005

Finished quilt size: 18˝ × 24˝

These baskets look like you could reach in and pick them up!

Materials

This is a scrappy quilt. Because it is small, it doesn't take much of any one fabric. Use the yardage amounts below as a guide. They will vary with the number of fabrics you use.

Green backgrounds: A variety of fabrics to total ⅝ yard

Purple strips: ⅛ yard

Appliqué and accent fabrics: A variety of scraps of fabric to total about ½ yard, including red for the accent strip

Binding: ⅔ yard

Backing and sleeve: ¾ yard

Batting: 24″ × 30″

Cutting

Refer to page 58 for color number references.

Green fabrics

1: Cut 1 square 7″ × 7½″.

2: Cut 2 rectangles 6½″ × 7½″.

3: Cut 1 square 6½″ × 6½″.

4: Cut 1 rectangle 8″ × 7½″.

5: Cut 1 rectangle 5½″ × 7½″.

6: Cut 1 rectangle 6″ × 6½″.

7: Cut 1 rectangle 5¾″ × 7½″.

9: Cut 1 strip 1¼″ × 7½″.

11: Cut 1 strip 3″ × 26½″.

13: Cut 1 strip 3½″ × 26½″.

Purple fabric

10: Cut 1 strip 1″ × 6½″.

12: Cut 1 strip 1½″ × 26½″.

Red accent fabric

8: Cut 2 strips 1″ × 7½″.

Binding

Cut 1 square 19″ × 19″ to make a 2½″-wide continuous bias strip 125″ long. (Refer to page 74 for instructions.)

Cut fabric for appliqué as needed.

Block Assembly

Refer to pages 64–69 for instructions on making the positioning overlay and preparing the appliqué. Use the Baskets appliqué pattern on page 16.

Baskets

1. Make 3 copies of the basket pattern.

2. Draw a rectangle 18″ × 24″ on a piece of paper.

3. Draw a center horizontal and vertical line.

4. Place the 3 basket patterns on the paper. Tape them in place.

5. Make the templates and positioning overlay from this paper pattern.

Background Block

The block is sewn together before the appliqué can be started. The outer edges will be trimmed after the appliqué is complete.

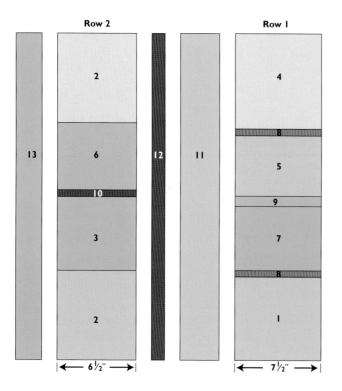

Background Assembly Diagram

1. Arrange cut pieces 1–13 on your design wall.

2. Sew the pieces together to form Row 1. Press toward the bottom.

3. Sew the pieces together to form Row 2. Press toward the bottom.

4. Sew strips 11 and 12 together lengthwise. Press toward 11.

5. Sew Row 1 to strip 12. Press toward 11.

6. Sew Row 2 to the other side of strip 12, as shown. Press toward 12.

7. Sew strip 13 to the left side of the quilt. Press toward 13.

8. Press the block in half horizontally and vertically to mark the center.

9. Appliqué the quilt.

10. After the appliqué is complete, press the quilt on the wrong side.

11. Trim the quilt to 18½″ × 24½″.

Quilting and Finishing

Refer to Quilting Techniques on pages 76–77. Refer to Finishing the Quilt on page 70 for layering, basting, and finishing.

1. You can mark quilting designs on the quilt top or plan to stitch without marking.

2. Layer and baste the quilt. Quilt by hand or machine.

3. Finish the quilt.

Log Cabin
Fragment

Made by Linda Jenkins, 2005

Finished quilt size: 16½″ × 57¾″

Linda made this quilt to use as a table runner. It would also be lovely hanging on a wall. Using a good range of greens is important in giving this quilt its luminous look.

Materials

This is a scrappy quilt. Use the yardage amounts below as a guide. They will vary with the number of fabrics you use.

Burgundy appliqué backgrounds and logs: ⅞ yard

Red logs: ⅓ yard

Grass green logs: ⅛ yard

Yellow-green logs: ⅛ yard

Dark yellow-green logs: ⅛ yard

Olive logs: ⅛ yard

Light olive logs: ⅛ yard

Blue-green logs: ⅛ yard

Light grass green logs: ⅛ yard

Dark grass green logs: ⅛ yard

Forest green logs: ⅛ yard

Appliqué fabrics: A variety of green scraps of fabric to total about ¼ yard

Binding: ⅝ yard

Backing and sleeve: 1¾ yards

Batting: 24″ × 65″

Cutting

Refer to page 61 for color letter references.

Burgundy fabric

Appliqué background: Cut 2 strips 10¼″ × 18½″.

Log Cabin blocks: Cut 8 strips 1¼″ × 40″. From these,

   A: Cut 10 squares 1¼″ × 1¼″.

   E: Cut 10 strips 1¼″ × 2¾″.

   H: Cut 10 strips 1¼″ × 3½″.

   M: Cut 10 strips 1¼″ × 5¾″.

   P: Cut 10 strips 1¼″ × 6½″.

   U: Cut 10 strips 1¼″ × 8¾″.

Red fabric

Cut 7 strips 1¼″ × 40″. From these,

   D: Cut 10 strips 1¼″ × 2″.

   I: Cut 10 strips 1¼″ × 4¼″.

   L: Cut 10 strips 1¼″ × 5″.

   Q: Cut 10 strips 1¼″ × 7¼″.

   T: Cut 10 strips 1¼″ × 8″.

Grass green fabric

Cut 2 strips 1¼″ × 40″. From these,

   B: Cut 10 squares 1¼″ × 1¼″.

   O: Cut 10 strips 1¼″ × 6½″.

Yellow-green fabric

Cut 1 strip 1¼″ × 40″. From this,

   C: Cut 10 strips 1¼″ × 2″.

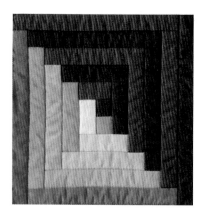

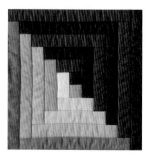

Dark yellow-green fabric

Cut 1 strip 1¼″ × 40″. From this,

F: Cut 10 strips 1¼″ × 2¾″.

Olive fabric

Cut 1 strip 1¼″ × 40″. From this,

G: Cut 10 strips 1¼″ × 3½″.

Light olive fabric

Cut 2 strips 1¼″ × 40″. From these,

K: Cut 10 strips 1¼″ × 5″.

Blue-green fabric

Cut 2 strips 1¼″ × 40″. From these,

J: Cut 10 strips 1¼″ × 4¼″.

Light grass green fabric

Cut 2 strips 1¼″ × 40″. From these,

N: Cut 10 strips 1¼″ × 5¾″.

Dark grass green fabric

Cut 2 strips 1¼″ × 40″. From these,

R: Cut 10 strips 1¼″ × 7¼″.

Forest green fabric

Cut 2 strips 1¼″ × 40″. From these,

S: Cut 10 strips 1¼″ × 8″.

Binding

Cut 1 square 22″ × 22″ to make a 2½″-wide continuous bias strip 180″ long. (Refer to page 74 for instructions.)

Cut fabric for appliqué as needed.

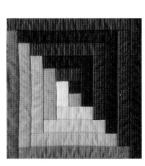

Block Assembly

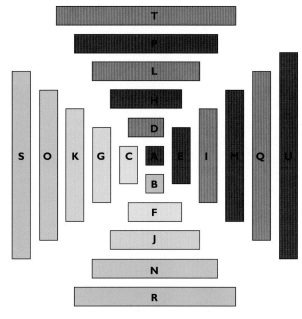

Block Assembly Diagram

Log Cabin Blocks

1. Arrange the strips in order from A to U.

2. Sew Square B to Square A. Press toward B.

3. Working in a clockwise rotation, sew Strip C to the block. Press toward C.

4. Continue working in a clockwise rotation. Sew the strips to the block in order. Press toward the newest strip.

5. The blocks should measure 8¾″ × 8¾″ unfinished. If they are not this size, you will need to adjust the size of the appliqué blocks.

Appliqué Blocks

Refer to pages 64–69 for instructions on making the positioning overlay and preparing the appliqué. The appliqué pattern for the Double Vine block is on the pullout at the back of the book.

1. Make the templates and the positioning overlay.

2. Appliqué the blocks.

3. After the appliqué is complete, press the blocks on the wrong side.

4. Trim the blocks to 8¾″ × 17″.

Quilt Assembly

Refer to the Quilt Assembly Diagram for quilt construction.

1. Arrange the Log Cabin blocks and appliqué blocks on your design wall.

2. Sew the Log Cabin blocks together into rows. Press toward the red.

3. Sew the rows together. Press toward the burgundy.

4. Sew a double vine block to each end. Press toward the double vine block.

Quilting and Finishing

Refer to Quilting Techniques on pages 76–77. Refer to Finishing the Quilt on page 70 for layering, basting, and finishing.

1. Quilt as desired. You can mark the quilting designs on the quilt top or plan to stitch without marking.

2. Layer and baste the quilt. Quilt by hand or machine.

3. Finish the quilt.

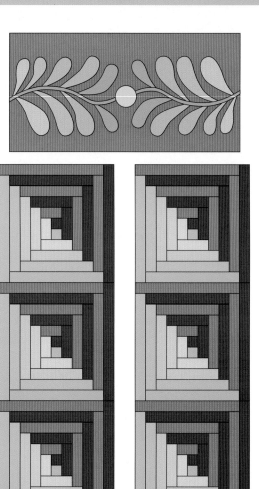

Quilt Assembly Diagram

We have a great way to do appliqué using sturdy laminated appliqué templates and a clear vinyl positioning overlay that makes it a snap to position all the pieces. If you're new to Piece O' Cake Designs appliqué techniques, read through all of these instructions before beginning a project.

For a more complete description of all our appliqué techniques, refer to our book *The New Appliqué Sampler* and our DVD *Learn to Appliqué the Piece O' Cake Way!*

Preparing the Backgrounds for Appliqué

Always cut the background fabric larger than the size it will be when it is pieced into the quilt. The outer edges of the block can stretch and fray as you handle it while stitching. The appliqué can shift during stitching and cause the block to shrink slightly. For these reasons it is best to add 1″ to all sides of the backgrounds when you cut them out. We have included this amount in the cutting instructions for each quilt. You will trim the blocks to size after the appliqué is complete.

1. Cut the backgrounds as directed in each project. For blocks with pieced backgrounds, cut and sew them together as directed.

2. Press each background block in half vertically and horizontally. This establishes a center grid in the background that will line up with the center grid on the positioning overlay. When blocks are symmetrically pieced, the seamlines are the grid lines, and you do not need to press creases for centering.

Press to create centering grid.

3. Use a pencil to draw a ¼″-long mark on each end of the pressed-in grid lines. Be sure not to make the lines too long or they will show on the block. These little lines will make it easier to correctly position the overlay as you work with it and will help you find the center when trimming the block.

4. Use a pencil to draw a little X in **one corner** of the block background. This X will be in the same corner as an X that you draw on the overlay. Be sure to mark the X near the edge so it won't show on the finished block.

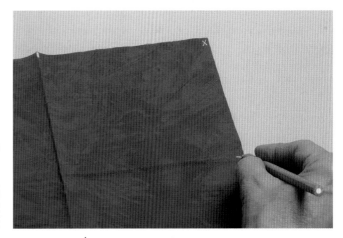

Draw ¼″-long lines at each end of pressed-in grid.
Draw small X in one corner.

Making the Appliqué Templates

Each appliqué shape requires a template, and we have a unique way to make templates that is both easy and accurate.

1. Use a photocopier to make 2–5 copies of each block. If the pattern needs to be enlarged, make the enlargement *before* making copies. Always compare the copies with the original to be sure they are accurate.

2. Cut out the appliqué shapes from these copies. Group them when you can—it saves on the laminate. Leave a little paper allowance around each shape or group. Where one shape overlaps another, cut the top shape from one copy and the bottom shape from another copy. You don't want a template with a hole in it!

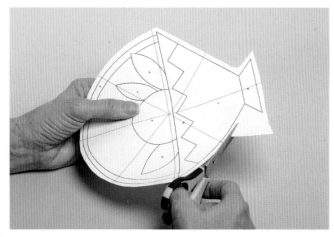

Cut out appliqué shapes.

3. Place a self-laminating sheet shiny side down on the table. Peel off the paper backing, leaving the sticky side of the sheet facing up.

4. If you are doing hand appliqué, place the templates *drawn* side down on the self-laminating sheet. For fusible appliqué, place the *blank* side down. Take care when placing each template onto the laminate. Use more laminating sheets as necessary.

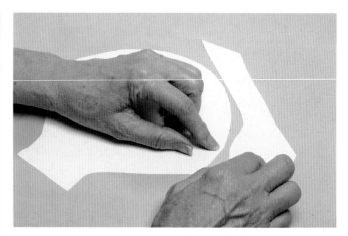

Place appliqué shapes *drawn* side down on self-laminating sheets for hand appliqué.

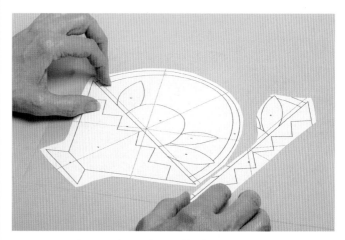

Place appliqué shapes *blank* side down on self-laminating sheets for fusible appliqué.

5. Cut out each shape. Try to split the drawn line with the scissors—don't cut inside or outside the line. Keep edges smooth and points sharp.

Cut out each template.

You'll notice how easy these templates are to cut out. That's the main reason we like this method. It is also true that a mechanical copy of the pattern is more accurate than hand tracing onto template plastic. As you use the templates, you will see that they are sturdy and hold up to repeated use.

Using the Templates for Hand Appliqué

For needle-turn hand appliqué, the templates are used right side up on the right side of the fabric. The templates are numbered. The numbers indicate the stitching sequence. You begin with Template #1 and work your way through the block.

1. Place the appliqué fabric right side up on a sandpaper board.

2. Place the template right side up (shiny laminate side up) on the fabric so that as many edges as possible are on the diagonal grain of the fabric. A bias edge is easier to turn under than one on the straight of grain.

3. Trace around the template. The sandpaper board will hold the fabric in place while you trace. Make a line you can see! Be sure to draw the line right up next to the edge of the template. It won't matter if the line is wide. It gets turned under.

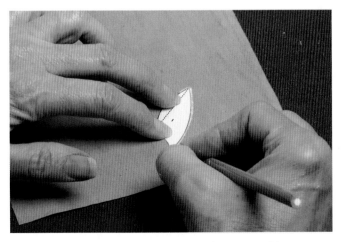

Place templates with as many edges as possible on bias, and trace around each template.

4. Cut out each piece, adding a $3/16''$ turn-under allowance.

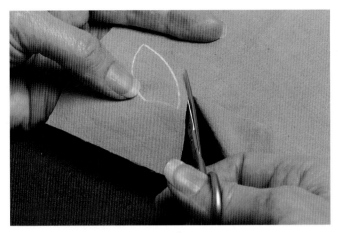

Cut out each piece, adding a $3/16''$ turn-under allowance.

Using the Templates for Fusible Appliqué

For fusible appliqué, templates are used with the drawn side down (shiny laminate side up) on the wrong side of the fabric. Use a nonstick pressing cloth to protect the iron and ironing board. Be sure to test the fabrics you plan to use.

We have reservations about recommending the use of fusible web. It is our opinion that this is not a good choice for an heirloom quilt. However, if you choose to use fusible web, follow the manufacturer's instructions.

1. Follow the manufacturer's instructions on the fusible web and iron it to the **wrong** side of the appliqué fabric. Do not peel off the paper backing.

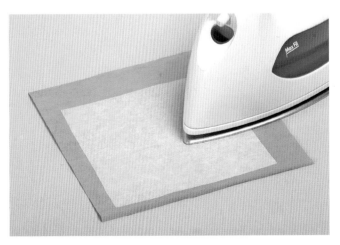

Iron fusible web to **wrong** side of fabric.

2. Leave the fabric right side down. Place the template drawn side down (shiny laminate side up) and trace around it onto the paper backing of the fusible web.

Trace around template onto paper backing.

3. Cut out the appliqué pieces on the drawn line. Add a scant ³⁄₁₆˝ allowance to any part of an appliqué piece that lies under another piece.

Cut out appliqué pieces.

4. Do not remove the paper backing until you are ready to position each piece on the block.

Making the Positioning Overlay

The positioning overlay is a piece of medium-weight clear upholstery vinyl that is used to position each appliqué piece accurately on the block. The overlay is easy to make and use, and it makes your projects portable.

You can find upholstery vinyl in a variety of places: quilt shops, other fabric shops, even hardware stores. It is 54˝ wide and comes on a roll with tissue paper. Keep the tissue paper! Buy clear vinyl that doesn't stretch easily and that can be pinned through.

1. Cut a piece of the upholstery vinyl, with its tissue paper lining, to the finished size of each block. Set the tissue paper aside until you are ready to fold or store the overlay.

2. Work directly from the patterns in this book or make a copy of them to work from. Enlarge as directed. Tape pattern pieces together as needed.

3. Tape the pattern onto a table.

4. Tape the upholstery vinyl over the pattern. Use a ruler and a Sharpie Ultra Fine Point Marker to draw the pattern's horizontal and vertical centerlines onto the vinyl.

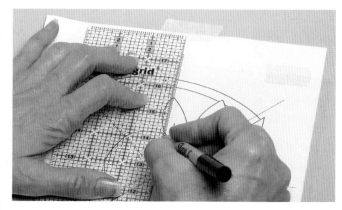

Tape vinyl over pattern and draw centerlines.

5. Accurately trace all the lines from the pattern onto the vinyl. The numbers on the pattern indicate the stitching sequence—include these numbers on the overlay. They also tell you which side of the overlay is the right side.

6. Draw a small X in one corner of the positioning overlay.

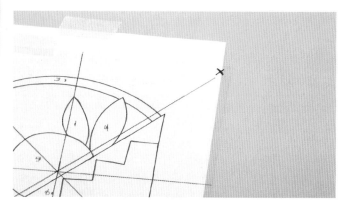

Trace pattern onto vinyl. Draw small X in one corner of overlay.

7. To store the overlay, place the tissue paper over the drawn side of the overlay and fold or roll the 2 pieces together.

Using the Positioning Overlay for Hand Appliqué

1. Place the background right side up on the work surface. We like to work on top of our sandpaper board. The sandpaper keeps the background from shifting as you position appliqué pieces on the block.

2. Place the overlay right side up on top of the background.

3. Line up the center grid line in the background with the center grid line of the overlay. Place the X on the overlay in the same corner as the X on the block.

4. Pin the overlay if necessary to keep it from shifting out of position. Flat, flower-head pins work best.

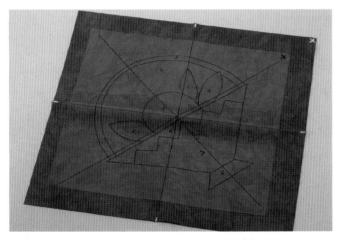

Place overlay on background and line up grid lines.

5. Before placing the appliqué pieces on the block, finger-press the turn-under allowances. **This is a very important step.** As you finger-press, make sure that the drawn line is pressed to the back. You'll be amazed at how much easier this one step makes needle-turning the turn-under allowance.

FINGER-PRESSING

It bears repeating: Finger-pressing is a very important step! You'll be amazed at how much easier this one step makes needle-turning the turn-under allowance.

Hold the appliqué piece right side up. Use your thumb and index finger to turn the turn-under allowance to the back of the appliqué so that the chalk line is just barely turned under. If you can see the chalk line on the top of the appliqué, it will be visible after it is sewn.

Use your fingers to press a crease into the fabric along the inside of the chalk line. Good-quality 100% cotton will hold a finger-press very well. Do not wet your fingers, use starch, or scrape your fingernail along the crease. Just pinch it with your fingertips. Finger-press every edge that will be sewn down.

Finger-press each piece with drawn line to back.

6. Place the first piece under the overlay but on top of the background. It is easy to tell when the appliqué pieces are in position under the overlay. As you work, finger-press and position one piece at a time. Be sure to place the appliqué pieces in numerical order.

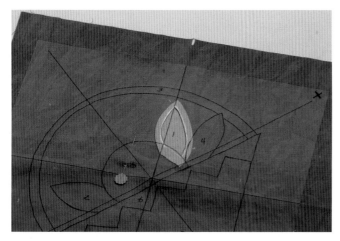

Use overlay to position appliqué pieces.

7. Fold back the overlay and pin the appliqué pieces in place using ½″ sequin pins. You can pin against the sand-paper board; doing so does not dull the pins. We usually position and stitch only 1 or 2 pieces at a time. Remove the vinyl overlay before stitching.

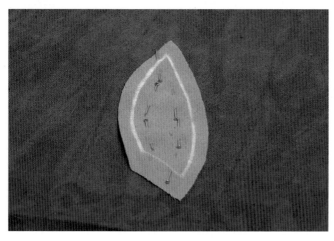

Pin appliqué piece in place.

8. Hand appliqué the pieces in place with an invisible stitch and matching thread.

9. When you are ready to put away the overlay, place the saved tissue paper over the drawn side before you fold it. The tissue paper keeps the lines from transferring from one part of the vinyl to another.

> **FOR YOUR INFORMATION**
> We don't trim the fabric behind our appliqué. We believe that leaving the background intact makes the quilt stronger. And, should the quilt ever need to be repaired, it's easier if the background has not been cut.

Using the Positioning Overlay for Fusible Appliqué

1. Place the background right side up on the ironing board.

2. Place the overlay right side up on top of the back-ground.

3. Line up the center grid line in the background with the center grid line of the overlay. Place the X on the overlay in the same corner as the X on the block.

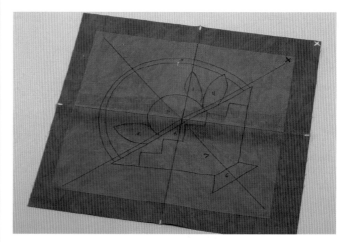

Place overlay on background and line up grid lines.

4. Peel off the paper backing from each appliqué piece as you go. Be careful not to stretch or ravel the outer edges.

5. Place the appliqué pieces right side up, under the overlay but on top of the background. Start with the #1 appliqué piece and follow the appliqué order. It is easy to tell when the appliqué pieces are in position under the overlay. You may be able to position several pieces at once.

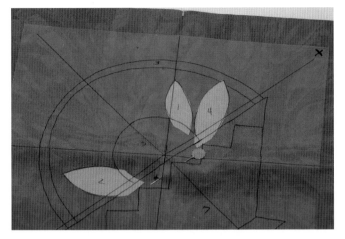

Use overlay to position appliqué pieces.

6. Carefully remove the overlay and iron the appliqué pieces in place. Be sure to follow the manufacturer's instructions for your brand of fusible web. Do not touch the overlay vinyl with the iron because the vinyl will melt.

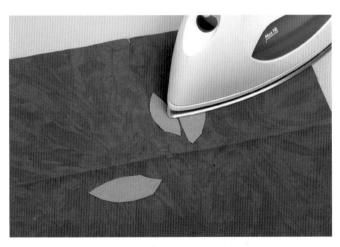

Fuse appliqué pieces in place.

7. After fusing cotton fabric, we recommend that you stitch around the edges of all fused appliqué pieces either by hand or machine. A blanket stitch in matching thread will lend a more traditional feel on these solid fabrics. As the quilts are used, the stitching keeps the edges secure.

Auditioning Your Fabric

We cut and place every fabric in position on the wall before we take a stitch! Always! By doing this we **know** that the quilt is going to be wonderful **before** putting all those stitches into it.

First put the backgrounds up on the design wall. If you are going to piece the backgrounds, put all the pieces on the wall. Sew the background blocks together only when you are sure they are balanced and work well together.

Starting with Block #1, trace and cut out the appliqué pieces. Start with whatever piece seems like the most obvious choice to you. Add the 3/16″ turn-under allowance and cut carefully. Use the overlay and place each piece on the wall as you go.

Each fabric is auditioning for its role in the quilt. Some fabrics are going to get the hook. Others will be perfect. You really don't know until you see them in place on the wall. **You can't fake the audition.** Sticking some fat quarters up on the wall and hoping for the best doesn't work. We know.

You will find out, as you read further, that some appliqué shapes are easier to sew if you cut them out leaving excess fabric around them. This is especially true with small, narrow, or pointy shapes. That means you won't get to use every appliqué piece that you have on the wall. Some will be sacrificed. But your quilts will be so much better if you audition every fabric.

When Block #1 is perfect, move on to Block #2. Continue until all the appliqué pieces are on the wall, even the borders. Place sashing strips, inner borders—everything that is part of that quilt—on the wall. Are you done?

Take a giant step back and really look at the quilt. Squint at it, use a reducing glass, take a picture—do whatever you need to do to help you evaluate the quilt. You are done when you are happy.

Pressing and Trimming the Blocks

Press the blocks on the wrong side after the appliqué is complete. If the ironing surface is hard, place the blocks on a towel so the appliqué will not get flattened. Be careful not to stretch the blocks as you press. Take your time when trimming the blocks to size. Be sure of the measurements **before** you cut. Remember to measure twice, cut once.

TRIMMING TIPS

Always look carefully at the block before you trim. We add 1″ to each side of the finished size of each block and border. You should be trimming off about ³/₄″ from each edge of the block. If you are set to trim much more (or less) than that, check the measurements.

Be sure that the appliqué is not too close to the edge of the block. Remember that there's a ¹/₄″ seam allowance. You don't want the appliqué in the seam!

Take your time. If it helps you to visualize how much you need to trim away, compare the paper pattern to the block.

1. Press the block on the wrong side.

2. Carefully trim each block to size. Measure from the center out, and always make sure the design is properly aligned before you cut off the excess fabric.

Finishing the Quilt

1. Assemble the quilt top following the instructions for each project.

2. Mark the quilt top for quilting (refer to pages 76–77).

3. Construct the back of the quilt, piecing as needed.

4. Place the backing right side down on a firm surface. Tape it down to keep it from moving around while you baste.

5. Place the batting over the backing and **pat** out any wrinkles.

6. Center the quilt top right side up over the batting.

7. Baste the layers together. Yes, we hand baste for both hand and machine quilting.

8. Quilt by hand or machine.

9. Trim the outer edges. Leave ¹/₄″–³/₈″ of backing and batting extending beyond the edge of the quilt top. This extra fabric and batting will fill the binding nicely.

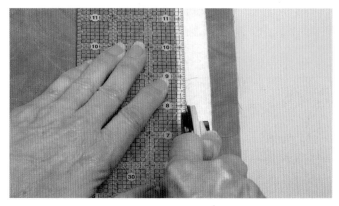

Trim outer edges.

10. Finish the outer edges with continuous bias binding. (Refer to pages 74–75.)

Making a Label and Sleeve

1. Make a hanging sleeve and attach it to the back of the quilt.

2. Make a label and sew it to the back of the quilt. Include information you want people to know about the quilt. Your name and address, the date, the fiber content of the quilt and batting, the name of the recipient or event if the quilt was made for a special person or occasion—these are all things that can go on the label.

Signing Your Quilt

You should always add a documentation patch to the back of your quilt. We have come to the conclusion that it's a good idea to get your name onto the front of the quilt as well. There are a variety of ways to do this.

You can appliqué your initials and the date on the quilt top. You can add information with embroidery or a permanent pen. Or you can quilt your name and the date into the quilt with matching or contrasting thread.

Cutaway Appliqué

The cutaway technique makes it much easier to stitch irregular, long, thin, or very small pieces. It is especially good to use for the stems in *Lorna's Vine* and the basket handles and pointed trim in *Baskets*.

1. Place the template on top of the selected fabric. Be sure to place the template on the fabric so that most of the edges will be on the diagonal grain of the fabric. Trace around the template.

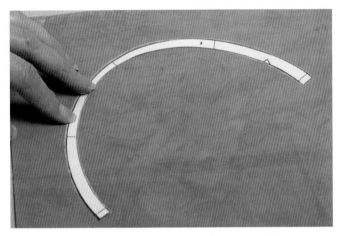

Place template with as many edges as possible on bias and trace around template.

2. Cut out the appliqué piece, leaving 1″ or more of excess fabric around the traced shape. Leave fabric intact in the V between points, inside deep curves, and so on.

3. Finger-press, making sure the drawn line is pressed to the back.

4. Use the vinyl positioning overlay to position the appliqué piece on the block.

5. Place pins ¼″ away from the finger-pressed edge. Place pins parallel to the edges. Large pieces, such as the basket handles, can be basted in place if you prefer. First pin the shape in place, then baste it. When a shape is curved, sew the concave side first if possible.

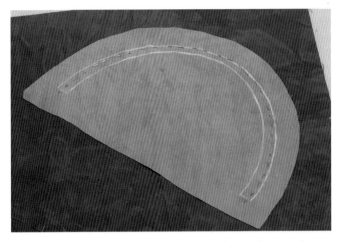

Pin appliqué piece in place. Baste large shapes if you prefer.

6. Begin trimming the excess fabric away from where you will start stitching, leaving a ³⁄₁₆″ turn-under allowance. Never start stitching at an inner or outer point that will be turned under.

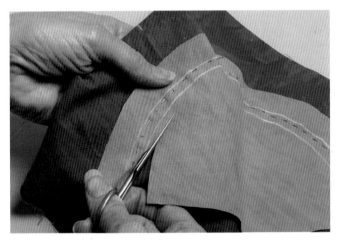

Cut away excess fabric and begin stitching.

7. Trim more fabric as you sew. Clip inner curves and inner points as needed.

8. Remove the pins as you stitch the next side of the piece. Trim excess fabric as necessary.

9. Continue until all sides of the appliqué piece are stitched.

Circle Appliqué

When sewing outer curves and circles, you can control only one stitch at a time. Use the needle or a round wooden toothpick to smooth out any pleats that form. Remember, the more you practice, the better you'll get.

1. Trace circles onto the selected fabric. Cut out each circle, adding a ³/₁₆″ turn-under allowance.

2. Finger-press the turn-under allowance, making sure the drawn line is pressed to the back.

3. Use the vinyl overlay to position the appliqué piece. Pin it in place. Use at least 2 pins to keep the circle from shifting.

4. Begin sewing. Turn under only enough turn-under allowance to take 1 or 2 stitches. If you turn under more, the appliquéd curve will have flat spaces and points.

Turn under only enough for 1 or 2 stitches.

5. Use the tip of the needle or a toothpick to reach under the appliqué to spread open any folds and to smooth out any points.

As seen from back: Use needle to open folds and to smooth points.

6. To close the circle, turn under the last few stitches all at once. The circle will tend to flatten out.

7. Use the tip of the needle to smooth out the pleats in the turn-under allowance and to pull the flattened part of the circle into a more rounded shape.

Off-the-Block Construction

Sometimes it is easier to sew appliqué pieces together "off the block" and then sew them as a unit to the block. Use this technique when appliqué pieces are stacked one on top of the other, as are the birds in *Birds of a Feather*.

1. Choose the fabrics that make up the appliqué. Trace around the templates onto the respective fabrics. Cut out the appliqué pieces, leaving enough excess fabric so the pieces are easy to hold on to.

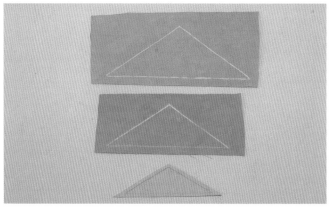

Trace and cut appliqué pieces.

2. In off-the-block construction you work from the top down. Appliqué Piece #3 is sewn to Piece #2. Finger-press it and position it over Piece #2. Pin it in place and sew it down.

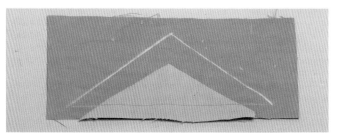

Work from top down. Sew Piece #3 to Piece #2.

3. Trim away the excess fabric from the newly created unit, leaving a ³/₁₆″ seam allowance. Finger-press and pin the #2/#3 unit to Piece #1. Sew it in place.

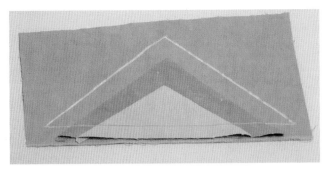

Sew #2/#3 unit to Piece #1.

4. Trim away the excess fabric from the newly created unit, leaving a ³⁄₁₆˝ seam allowance. Finger-press and pin the unit to the block.

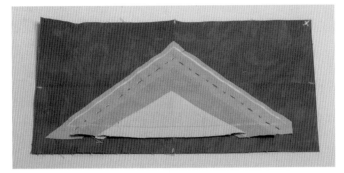

Sew unit to block.

Making Continuous Bias Stems

This is a great technique for stems that are uniform in width. It is also good for very long stems—such as the vine in the border of *Feathers*.

You will need a package of bias bars to make these bias stems. Each package contains a variety of bar widths. This technique can be used for any width bias stem that you have a corresponding bias bar for. We like the heat-resistant plastic bars. You may also find metal Celtic bars that work the same way.

1. Make a continuous bias strip 1½˝ wide. (Refer to page 74 for instructions.) Lightly press the strip in half lengthwise with the wrong sides together.

2. Place the folded edge of the bias strip along the correct line on the seam guide of the sewing machine (for ¼˝ stems, use the ¼˝ line). Before you sew too far, insert the bias bar into the open end to make sure it fits. Sew the length of the bias strip.

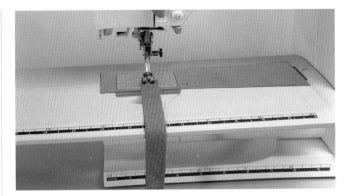

Place folded edge of bias strip along correct line on sewing machine seam guide.

3. Trim away the excess fabric, leaving a very scant seam allowance.

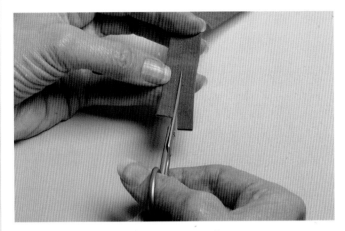

Trim, leaving scant seam allowance.

4. Insert the appropriate size bias bar into the sewn bias tube. Shift the seam to the back of the bar and press it in place. Move the bias bar down the tube, pressing as you go.

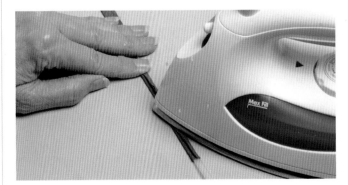

Press using bias bar.

5. Hold up the finished bias stem. Notice that it curves more in one direction than the other. The side closest to the seamline makes the tighter curve. When possible, match this side of the bias stem to the concave side of the stem on the pattern.

Making Continuous Bias Binding

We find this method for making continuous bias to be particularly easy. A surprisingly small amount of fabric makes quite a bit of bias, and there is no waste. We show you how to master those tricky binding corners on the next page.

We normally make our binding strips 2½″ wide.

1. Start with a square of fabric and cut it in half diagonally. Refer to the pattern for the size of the square.

2. Sew the 2 triangles together, right sides together, as shown. Be sure to sew the edges that are on the straight of grain. If you are using striped fabric, match the stripes. You may need to offset the fabric a little to make the stripes match.

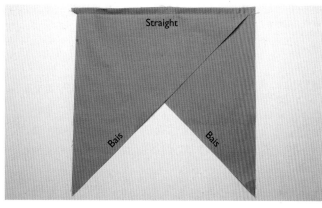

Sew straight-of-grain edges of triangles together.

3. Press the seam allowances open. Measure 2½″ into each side as shown and make a short cut parallel to the bias edge of the tube.

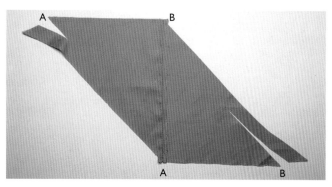

Make short cut 2½″ wide.

BIAS STEM TIP

When making continuous bias to be used in bias stems, don't press the seam allowances open. Instead, press them to one side. There are 2 seams. Make sure that they are both pressed in the **same** direction. When you run the bias bar through the fabric, you'll be happy the seams are all going the same way!

When making a continuous bias strip for stems, cut the strip 1½″ wide.

4. Match the A's and B's with the fabric right sides together. Pin and sew. Press the seam open.

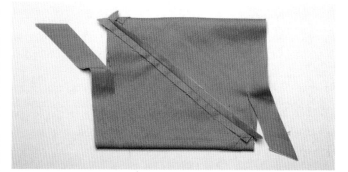

Pin and sew. Press.

5. Use a rotary cutter and ruler to cut the continuous bias strip 2½″ wide.

6. Press the length of the bias strip wrong sides together for double-fold binding.

CONTINUOUS BIAS CUTTING TIP

Try putting a small cutting mat on the end of the ironing board. Slide the tube of fabric over the mat. Use a ruler and rotary cutter to cut a long strip of continuous bias, rotating the tube of fabric as needed. Cut using gentle pressure—if the ironing board is padded, the cutting surface may give if you press very hard.

Sewing Binding to the Quilt

1. Cut the first end of the binding at a 45° angle. Turn under this end ½″ and press.

2. Press the continuous binding strip in half lengthwise, wrong sides together.

3. With raw edges even, pin the binding to the edge of the quilt, beginning a few inches away from a corner. Start sewing 6″ from the beginning of the binding strip, using a ¼″ seam allowance.

4. Stop ¼″ away from the corner and backstitch several stitches.

Stop ¼″ away from corner. Backstitch.

5. Fold the binding straight up as shown. Note the 45° angle.

Fold binding up.

6. Fold the binding straight down and begin sewing the next side of the quilt.

Fold binding down and begin sewing.

7. Sew the binding to all sides of the quilt, following the process in Steps 4–6. Stop a few inches before you reach the beginning of the binding, but don't trim the excess binding yet.

8. Overlap the ends of the binding and cut the second end at a 90° angle. *Be sure to cut the binding long enough so the cut end is covered completely by the angled end.*

9. Slip the 90° end into the angled end.

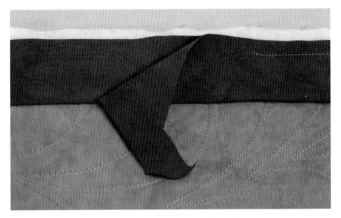

Slip 90° end into angled end.

10. Pin the joined ends to the quilt and finish sewing the binding to the quilt.

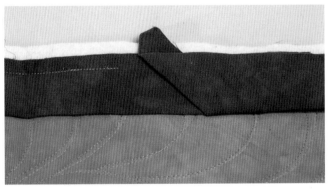

Pin and finish sewing.

11. Turn the binding to the back of the quilt, covering the raw edges. If there is too much batting, trim some to leave the binding nicely filled. Hand stitch the folded edge of the binding to the back of the quilt.

Quilting Techniques

Quilting really shows on solid fabrics! There is no pattern in the cloth to hide the stitches. It is important to carefully consider the quilting pattern before you begin to mark and quilt.

Traditional Amish quilting designs are just that—traditional. Lines and grids, both straight and at an angle, are very common. A wide variety of feathered designs can be found—vines, wreaths, feather segments, and so on. Chains, fans, interlocking circles, fruit baskets, simple flowers—you will see all of these. You won't see much stippling. In fact, we can't remember seeing any stippling in antique Amish quilts.

Traditional Amish quilts are not as heavily quilted as many quilts are today. They were hand quilted! The women who made them had neither the time nor the inclination to do lots of heavy hand quilting.

Hand-quilted quilts in general drape differently than heavily machine-quilted quilts do. When you quilt by hand, you have one thread that goes up and down through the layers, holding them together. The spaces between the stitches give the quilt a softer drape—even with heavy hand quilting.

When you quilt on the sewing machine, there are two tracks of thread—one that runs above the quilt and another that runs below. Each stitch cinches the layers tightly together. The more quilting you put into the quilt, the "harder" the quilt becomes.

Some traditional Amish quilts have areas that are unquilted. Because they are hand quilted and have a softer look, these areas without quilting are fine. Machine quilting, in contrast, pulls the layers together more emphatically, making areas without quilting look baggier.

We wanted to preserve the design sensibilities of the traditional Amish quilts *and* we also wanted to machine quilt our quilts. That meant that the quilting lines in our quilts needed to be a little closer together than those seen in the older Amish quilts. We didn't feel that stippling of

any sort looked Amish. We opted instead for lines, grids, and echo quilting in our backgrounds. The quilting motifs we chose are traditional—with the occasional contemporary twist thrown in!

Making Stencils

We make stencils in much the same way we make appliqué templates.

1. Use a photocopier to make 1 copy of the stencil pattern. If the stencil pattern is larger than a sheet of paper, tape copies together to make the entire pattern. Always compare the copies with the original to be sure they are accurate.

2. Place a self-laminating sheet shiny side down on the table. Peel off the paper backing, leaving the sticky side of the sheet facing up. Place the pattern **drawn** side down on the self-laminating sheet. If the pattern is large, use more laminating sheets as necessary.

Place pattern **drawn** side down on self-laminating sheet.

3. Trim the stencil sheet to the size indicated by the box around it on the pattern.

4. Place the stencil on a rotary cutting mat. Use an X-ACTO knife to cut the stencil. Cut along the edges of the wide lines. You will be left with channels in the stencil to draw through. Be sure to leave bridges between cuts so that the stencil does not fall apart.

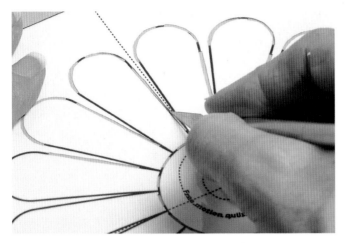

Cut out lines with X-ACTO knife.
Leave bridges between cuts.

5. Use the dashed centerlines on the pattern to help you position the stencil on the quilt.

DELEGATE!

There are some jobs that are nice to delegate! Cutting stencils can be hard on your fingers. Becky persuaded her son Jeff to cut her stencils. She freely admits that he did a much better job than she would have. They had a nice visit while he was working, and her hands were saved.

Too often we think that only *we* can do the job correctly. Paul, Linda's husband, is a great baster. Becky's husband, Steve, sews binding down like a pro. Each of these men feels a sense of satisfaction, we're proud of them, *and* we get to do something we like better. It's all good.

Marking Your Quilt

Mark quilts lightly before you layer and baste the three layers together. The pencils we use most often are listed in Basic Supplies on page 6. **Always** test your pencil on scrap fabric to make sure that it will come out later.

Only mark what you have to. For example, Becky quilted strips of feathers between lines of channel quilting in the borders of *Birds of a Feather*. She marked the straight lines of the channel quilting but not the feathers. That left her with fewer pencil marks to remove later.

Birds of a Feather quilting detail

BE CAREFUL!

Never heat set a mark into a quilt! Do not iron over a mark that you want to remove later. Be careful how you handle the quilt-in-progress. Never leave it in a hot car for any length of time.

Quilting

Use the best equipment that you can afford. When hand quilting, that means having a good hoop or frame. There are some great thimbles to choose from too. As your hands change with time, keep your thimble up to date.

Successful machine quilting requires the best sewing machine and table that you can afford. We love our Berninas! We love the large tables that our machines fit down into too. The table supports the weight of the quilt. Having the work surface level with the bed of the sewing machine means more even stitches and less wear and tear on your arms.

Quilting gloves allow you to move the quilt without so much strain on your hands.

Change your needle often.

Use good thread for both hand and machine quilting. When machine quilting, we use the same thread that we recommend for hand appliqué. We generally match the thread color to the color of the fabric in the quilt top. As we move from color to color, we change the thread color. Whatever color we are using on top is used in the bobbin.

The key to good stitches—by both hand and machine—is practice.

About the Authors

The Green Country Quilter's Guild in Tulsa, Oklahoma, can be credited with bringing Linda Jenkins and Becky Goldsmith together. Their friendship developed while they worked together on many guild projects, and through a shared love for appliqué. This partnership led to the birth of Piece O' Cake Designs in 1994, and survived Linda's move to Pagosa Springs, Colorado, and then back to Tulsa in 2001, while Becky headed for Sherman, Texas.

Linda owned and managed a beauty salon before she started quilting. Over the years she developed a fine eye for color as a hair colorist and makeup artist. Becky's degree in interior design and many art classes provided a perfect background for quilting. Linda and Becky have shown many quilts and have won numerous awards. Together they make a dynamic quilting duo and love to teach other quilters the joys of appliqué.

In the fall of 2002 Becky and Linda joined the C&T Publishing family, where they continue to produce wonderful books and patterns.

Look for more Piece O' Cake books from C&T Publishing.

For more information about individual Piece O' Cake patterns, contact C&T Publishing.

Resources

Piece O' Cake Designs
www.pieceocake.com

**Cherrywood Fabrics
(hand-dyed fabric)**
P.O. Box 486
Brainerd, MN 56401
888-298-0967
www.cherrywoodfabrics.com

For More Information
Ask for a free catalog:
C&T Publishing, Inc.
P.O. Box 1456
Lafayette, CA 94549
800-284-1114
email: ctinfo@ctpub.com
website: www.ctpub.com

Quilting Supplies
Cotton Patch Mail Order
3404 Hall Lane
Dept. CTB
Lafayette, CA 94549
800-835-4418 925-283-7883
email: quiltusa@yahoo.com
website: www.quiltusa.com

Note: Fabrics used in the quilts shown may not be currently available, as fabric manufacturers keep most fabrics in print for only a short time.

Index

Useful Information

Projects

Great Products from C&T PUBLISHING

3-in-1 NEW & IMPROVED COLOR TOOL

NEW & IMPROVED 3-in-1 COLOR TOOL

NOW INCLUDES THESE MUST-HAVE TOOLS!
- *Numbered Swatches*
- *Two Value Finders Green and Red*

PLUS
- *Color Guide*
- *Fabric Preview Windows*

IDEAL FOR:
Quilting
Crafts
Home décor
Knitting
Sewing
Scrapbooking
Floral design
Graphic design!

JOEN WOLFROM

AN AMISH ADVENTURE

A Workbook for Color in Quilts

Second edition

Roberta Horton

Beautifully Quilted with Alex Anderson

• How to Choose or Create the Best Designs for Your Quilt

- Full-size Patterns, Ready to Use
- 5 Timeless PROJECTS

Host of Simply Quilts seen on HGTV

250 Continuous-Line QUILTING DESIGNS

for Hand, Machine & Long-Arm Quilters

Laura Lee Fritz

HARRIET HARGRAVE HEIRLOOM MACHINE QUILTING

Comprehensive Guide to Hand-Quilted Effects
Using Your Sewing Machine

REVISED AND EXPANDED THIRD EDITION

GWEN MARSTON Classic Four-Block Appliqué Quilts

A BACK-TO-BASICS APPROACH